# BENZEDRINE HIGHWAY

by

## CHARLES PLYMELL

KICKS BOOKS

NEW YORK, NEW YORK

I

Published in 2013 by Kicks Books
PO Box 646 Cooper Station
New York NY 10276

Printed in the United States of America

ISBN: 978-1-940157-99-3

Editor: Miriam Linna
Design: Patrick Broderick/Rotodesign

www.kicksbooks.com

### BILLY THE KID
### GOT NOTHING ON ME
### CUSTER WAS A LOSER, TOO

Buck toothed twisted mind from
Punk long ago in Hell's Kitchen
Eighteen Hundred Seventy-Seven
The System made him run and kill
The House holds the cards like always
Every rider every year kids up and go
Got the god particle in pocket need more
Sweet Mother I can no longer mind the store
Earth's dark soul put a bullet in the chamber.

Billy Bonney rode a good horse, a Paint
No chrome off Pontiac Bonneville Eight
Rt 66 to hook up with the Santa Fe Trail
Beware of Pat Garrett a sneak and ferret
He's part of the house, part system, future
To lock up all the lone horseman, a game
Out gunned by part jerk, part fuzz, part fink
Joker of life up his sleeve like entropy kink
Be careful dark rider he likes gun in hand
Like his ilk killed the buffalo, killed the land
Killed the innocent spirit yearning to be true.

# PRAISE FOR PLYMELL

"Spun out of that vortex which is Wichita, Charley Plymell reached San Francisco on that road that ran thru the astonished heart of America, riding his chopper (at least in my imagined midnight cowboy movie of him)— Kansas madman's dream, eternity in the groin— Neal Cassady, down, Kerouac down, all down the Great American Drain—and the vision goes on—"
—*Lawrence Ferlinghetti*

"From the first paragraph the reader is drawn into the writer's space. Plymell has as much in depth to say about death as Hemingway did and a lot more to say about in terms of the present generation stillborn into a world that can offer nothing...death from an OD...Death from a plane crash...Computerized death...He is saying a lot about life which becomes the chewed over leftovers of death... 'A manifesto of ashes' A very readable manifesto."
—*William S. Burroughs*

"The book made me think of both: *Tropic of Cancer* and *Naked Lunch* with maybe a little of *Castle to Castle* for good measure which is to say that you've got a lot going for you in your own voice. Keep 'em flying."
—*Tom Wolfe*

"Better that Desolation Angels."
—*Claude Pelieu*

# INTRODUCTION

## BY

## CHARLES PLYMELL

I was born in April 1935, during the blackest
dust storm ever to hit Holcomb, Kansas. We
lived in a converted chicken coop—Mother,
Father, four older sisters and I. No electricity.
We staved off hunger, eating fried cactus and
jackrabbits that Mother would shoot with her
.22 Remington Pump that she had ordered from
the Sears catalogue. It replaced her keen arrow.
Sometimes we shared our "Hoover steaks" with
hoboes off the rails. Her great-grandmother had
been on the Trail of Tears. On my father's side,
the Bohemian Plymells had come over in the
1600's, worked westward, married a Wyandotte
before that tribe came to Kansas City and bought
land from the Crows, Rattlebone Flats and all.

My father, as a young cowboy, trailed cattle
to Galveston and had hired out on a ship to Italy
before coming back to homestead in outlaw
country No Man's Land before it became a state.
When it did, my father did time in the Oklahoma
State Prison. The Territory was a haven for
outlaw riders of the purple sage. A lifetime later,
William S. Burroughs would admire the rifle
while sighting it in his Sears Roebuck cottage
in Lawrence, Kansas. He said, "They don't make
them like this anymore. Feel it, Charley — just
like a woman's leg."

I was about five years old when the family
picked up and headed west on Route 66 in our

International truck bed with its dually tires singing down the highway, much like *The Boxcar Children*, the first prose book I read. We traveled from Kansas and Oklahoma to Yucaipa, California, a place that I remember as paradise, the Los Angeles basin before it was spoiled. My sisters set up a basement school for my kindergarten year. I think my dad was on the road, trucking, or maybe working on the railroad at that time. I remember playing in my aunt's orange grove while ripe navel oranges fell to the ground plentifully. If a tramp came by, he had a treat. I remember the flowing creek of pure water to drink, and the pastel-colored rocks, beautiful and shiny, the smell of orange blossoms filling the air. Even the pavement glistened. I wouldn't experience such vibrant awareness again until I ingested the magic chemistry in San Francisco in 1963.

We went back to the Dust Bowl where the homestead was, the Palo Apache land that President Grover Cleveland had given my grandfather, Charley Plymell, who ran his stageline west of Dodge City and south to the Territory. I wanted to give it back to the Apache, but my born-again sisters saw its future as God's "growth" of the fossil fuel/energy curse that would rape the land and leave the cows bawling for good water. Poachers, more lowdown than rattlers, would kill anything that moved with their high caliber weapons. While Dillinger set the ethos for the day, we were readers, singers, and philosophers. My mother would play her guitar and sing Jimmy Rodgers and Woody Guthrie songs. While riding on the prairie one day, my dad said whoever or whatever was behind it all wasn't going to let a little thing like Man figure it out, and that he would just go mad trying. That became my philosophy in later years. My literary influence was closer to the poet Lucretius. In this, my dad had instilled in me a healthy skepticism for anyone who claimed to know the path or how to govern the masses. He went back to farming. I would sit in the truck and wait, while my dad on a tractor and plow, and my mother on the same, would disappear toward the horizon, and fade into space. When they had to change fields a few miles down the road, Dad put the truck in gear and jumped out, leaving me behind the wheel. I had to stand up to see where I was going. I was then about six years old.

That truck was my studio. I stood in it, singing, gearshift knob as microphone, lines from a Hank Williams radio show or maybe Roy Acuff. I sang as loud as I could into endless space: "I'm just a happy rovin' cowboy/ Herding the dark clouds out of the sky/ Deep in the heavens blue." Song and existential dust in the vast cyclonic prairie. My father invited Mexican railroad crews of gandy dancers to come over to our house, play guitars and sing happy songs with their bright-eyed children. Good weed grew along the tracks.

My parents divorced. My father sold the land, the best wheat land in the world with oil and gas under it. He went back to looking for the perfect cattle ranch of his dreams. He looked all over the West and in Costa Rica, Australia, and South America. He would come home with senoritas, but there were times we didn't see him for a while.

My mother got the short end, of course, in those days. She worked slinging hash in Ulysses, Kansas during the war, more for the social life if anything. *The Soldier's Last Letter* played on the jukebox. She did the best she could, and got a job in Fraser, Colorado. I faked eating chicken-fried steak while slipping the slippery slabs in my pocket. She later worked in aircraft factories in Wichita, and she was a stunt driver in an Auto Thrill Show in Oklahoma where I joined her in a '48 Dodge I drove from South Dakota where my dad had land. There was no such thing as a driver's license in that state. That was in 1948/49.

Dad turned up now and again between Pan-Am flights. He had trucked for Riss and Company during the Depression along Route 66 from Chicago to L.A. In Chicago, someone put a gun in his back and escorted him to the voting booth. Later on the farm, he went back to Chicago and bought a 1939 Buick with tire mounts, and a window behind the driver's seat and a gearshift on the floor. He added it to our cars in Kansas that my sisters and I would steal to take on spins. Also a baby blue 1940 Packard, like a general's car, a sweet 1940 Chevy coupe, and a 1940 V-8 Ford coupe, like Dillinger preferred. I helped drive the '39 Buick gangster car up to the Continental Divide at Fraser where my mother worked at a cabin camp café and bar. With the big straight 8 and a stick shift on the floor, it was no strain even loaded down. At that, it got 25 miles to the gallon at 25 cents a gallon, no testament to the criminal enterprise conspiracy of fossil fuels.

Before they divorced, my folks hit a few good years with wheat crops. For ten grand cash, my father bought a nice little modern brick ranch home with a large garden tract out back that ended on the banks of the Little Arkansas in Wichita. I went to junior high school there, driving to California and back on my Benzedrine Highway many times over the coming years. My dad had put me in a private military academy in San Antonio during my last year of junior high. He thought I might become a jet ace. It sounded good to me. I fell asleep on the drive down there while listening to *The Tennessee Waltz* on the car radio. He left for South America, and after I left military school that year, he bought me a brand-new 1951 Chevrolet that I drove to Blythe, California border where he had some land on the Colorado River.

I'd drive to LA, to Old Mexico, to pick up some criss-cross bennies, and back via Route 66 to Wichita and K.C.and back via the Benny Highway to Wichita and KC, hitting the niteclubs across the tracks where the real combos played to their people.  I had a '32 hotrod Ford and bought a new '52 Chevy coupe. I was a street hipster and was supposed to begin my freshman year in high school in Wichita. I lasted a month and with gas at fifteen cents a gallon, and a new car and jobs whenever I wanted to work, I thought school a waste of time as I wandered the western states, riding in rodeos, working in the fields.

There were a lot of clubs then where the greats sang to small crowds for a dollar cover charge. In my Pontiac with the chrome chief on hood and Hank Ballard and the Midnighters on the radio, Annie didn't work with me on that trip to Joplin, MO. No mo. In the Ducktail days, we hipsters had a lot of musician friends who would take us to the all-night clubs across the tracks. We could also see the greatest in hillbilly bands before they became commercial country. They had mason jars of Benzedrine and Dexedrine.

The drugs of the day were Bennies & Boo. We'd go to clubs in K.C. where almost a decade earlier Jay McShann and teenage Charlie Parker came down to Wichita to the Trocadero Club and played *Wichita Blues*. The cover charge was fifty cents after midnight. The first known recording of Charlie Parker was made in Wichita in 1940. I met Fats Domino after he had driven to the Mambo Club across the tracks in his '49 Caddy coupe with the bass tied on top to play for a handful of people. We didn't even go outside to smoke. That was before *Blueberry Hill*. I was a solid street hipster seeing the greats of jazz & race and R&B like the multitudes today going to concerts, but a two drink cover charge and a friend from across the tracks would get us into all the clubs to hear the greats who white folks wouldn't know about until decades later.

I bought a 1950 Olds 88 convertible, the hottest rocket on wheels. My Rocket 88! A friend and I got on the Benny Highway to Bakersfield to go over to Oildale (across the tracks for Okies) to a notorious club that Buck Owens and Merle Haggard were said to frequent. We scored some crisscross Bennies, and I went into L.A. up on the hill above the Angel's Flight where fights and boo and dance kicked up the existential dust in downtown L.A. Then, I headed to my dad's cantaloupe farm in Blythe on the Colorado River. He didn't like my car and traded it in on a new GMC pickup for me. I turned up the radio and parked on downtown streets. Johnny Ray was singing *Cry*.

I went to Hollywood and traded the pickup in on a new 1953 Buick Roadmaster Riviera, and drove it up to Oregon. I picked crops; worked a union job on the Dalles dam on the Columbia

River. Bought a little tugboat for a cabin. I turned on the radio. Johnny Ace was singing *The Clock*. I heard Rose Maddox. I drove on. I headed back to Wichita across Nevada at a 100 mph alone, no lights on the horizon, or in the sky. I'd switch the lights off, and it was dark as void... then all of a sudden in the black night, I saw what they all say they were seeing at that time — the cigar-shaped mother ship and a few saucers flying out of it. My neck tingled, and I put that straight eight to the floor to a hundred and ten, but then realized the saucers were going in another direction, so I turned on the radio. Hank Williams gave me some comfort singing the lonesome song he could have heard in his own '52 baby blue Cadillac convertible with continental kit.

On our own, for our own kicks, not because of any other culture but hip, we were reading Ezra Pound and Henry Miller when a fellow hipster convinced me to matriculate at what was then Wichita University. Lord Buckley and Professor Longhair were our teachers when few wild outcasts got a taste of higher education mixed with hipster nightlife in the 50's. We took peyote on the same riverbanks as the Kansa tribes had since time began, and then Route 66 again to L.A. and El Camino Real to San Francisco in the early 60's. I rode with my oldest sister who knew all the madams in the Northwest and who worked as a prostitute until she ended up in San Francisco too, where she died on the street in the Mission District. I had worked on the docks in San Francisco while living with my sister and Frank in the Tenderloin. Frank was the offspring of the white sheriff and the black madam of Deadwood, South Dakota, a very likeable guy who got me in the Union. It was the best pay and best benefits anyone could have. There were no co-pays. The bill was always zero for the best dentist we could find, best doctor at Kaiser or anywhere, free prescriptions, free eyeglasses. Once my crew boss stopped me while working and said: "Hey Plymell, you know the mob owns the company and owns the Union too?" "Yeah, sure, the best organized government in the country." I was O.K. with them from then on.

I met Ginsberg, Whalen, McClure, and Ferlinghetti when they came to a party I was having at my flat on Gough Street with Glenn Todd and Dave Haselwood from Wichita, who were involved in poetry and publishing. I had learned to run an offset press while going to college in Wichita and started printing little mags in S. F. around 1963. Neal Cassady and Allen Ginsberg moved into the Gough Street flat to share it with me. I had moved there from my earlier pad in 1962 on the corner of Haight and Ashbury. It was a nice Russian working-class neighborhood, but the hippies had started to move in daily, and I mean really daily. The Beats wanted to integrate with the new "heads" we called them, later to be called hippies & yippies. City Lights published my poems. So did Poetry, Chicago, Paris Review, Evergreen Review, and the like. In '66, Dave Haselwood published my first collection of poetry, *Apocalypse Rose*, in book form. By the time City Lights published my Hobohemian collage prose book *The Last Of The Moccasins*, Neal had gone off with Ken Kesey and Tom Wolfe on his "Furthur" bus for acid trips. I'd been collaborating with William Burroughs on some cut-up writings we were sending to each other. He was living in England at the time. Allen Ginsberg wrote an introduction to my first book and Ferlinghetti wrote one for my second book, so, I was associated with the Beats in literature, but my interests were also in music and later the Underground Comix. When Robert Crumb came to town, I printed his first ZAP, later to be tagged by collectors as "the Plymell ZAP", and I had printed the first S. Clay Wilson in Lawrence, KS, where we had lived before he came to S.F. and became involved with ZAP.

*Apocalypse Rose* appears in print here again, at last, with *The Last Of The Moccasins*, and a selection of prophetic random poetic outbursts. These are the writings of the great years for me, never to happen again. It's dedicated to Johnny Ace, Hank Williams, Charlie Parker, Fats Domino, Lightnin' Hopkins, Wilbert Harrison, Link Wray, Hasil Adkins, and all the junkies, psychos, teamsters, freaks, con men, criminals, artists, poets, queens, cops, cowboys, truckers, and little old ladies who've made the trip with me on the *Benzedrine Highway*.

—*Charles Plymell*

# APOCALYPSE ROSE

### FOREWORD
BY ALLEN GINSBERG

# FOREWORD

Plymell and his friends inventing the Wichita *Vortex* contribute to a tradition stretching back from Lamantia thru Sherwood Anderson to Poe and earlier American vibration artists of these provinces. A decade earlier than Plymell that same death vibration had driven a host of prophetic youths out of heartland Kansas — Bruce Connor arrived on both oceans with combines, instant movies, placards, paintings & married hair; Brakhage retired to rough mountains for his solitary eye-perceptions; Bob Branaman matures in Big Sur one of the most exquisite visionary painters in America; McClure flourishes a terrific poet roaring sensibly in San Francisco.

The *Vortex* vibration is in these Apocalypse Rose writings — unearthly hum of a tornado of conscious droning in on a brain born to provincial solitude, perverted local politics, sick police, ignoble State College bureaucracies, reactionary airplane money real estate, blackout of Whitman's blissful Adhesiveness among Citizens. Hermaphrodite among the Birchites! Good God! A miracle of humanity therefore the unconditional early lyric expression "fresh, sweet, like Kid Cupid's slim ovaries."

That poem has quality similar to Hart Crane quatrain — moonbeam compressed in iron lines. A puzzling original gift, that can create classic style revised-concentration verse – like scripture including New Conscious Martian radio messages and amphetamine babble. Plymell has old fashioned modesty & hesitancy toward Poetry, a sentimental regard to eliminate

1

passages that don't glisten & zing; what's left is
a residue of awkwardly pure high "poems." This
*literary* peculiarity — a single man's idea of Art
still cherished as might've been fantasied in teen
age provinces — is an Ideal offering by a man
lone in fear — I feel respect for True & Honest
character in these exact terms.

That's general; what's exactly interesting
are the images present in the book in all their
Midwestern mysteriousness, Catherine, with
your metal sandwich?...your hero in black
sculpture spurs...nights n K.C./Jr. gangsters,
Jazz and Mr. B Collars...I'm singing the Great
Speckle Bird...in a ragged chartreuse Ford...
moon on the dashboard...O Radar Queen in
Compton's...perhaps no nearer to panorama
than thou...all night movies on the meat block/
where teen age...Acid spreaders/burned my
ovaries with a sunlamp...the brain watchers
predicted/I would be in the fields...O flappy
blue...caught in the feigning/of wheat and honey
bee...where early frost stigmata...chasing
Einstein, shouting/questions with a Kansas
twang...Joyous supernal they sit on a weed.

A lot of sweet lines are remarked in Rimbaud
& Crane & sometimes pierce through Lowell's
poems. I interpret his statement as prophetic
fragment memory of innocence, visionary great
fear, & Warm glimmer : a new species?

—*Allen Ginsberg*
October 28, 1966

## APOCALYPSE ROSE

The Juke-box begins its song:
futuristic mirage blossom
dimensions of accelerated fortune tellers.
Leaving his coffee,
the boy from nowhere
dials any combination of numbers
on the telephone,
smiles under the beat
of NOWHERE TO HIDE.
The night that shades his darkened eyes
unwinds into mistaken paradise.
Numbed with gravity
the song grows fainter.
those closer to the earth
are last to go.
Image passed on streets long vacant.

The hand that strikes the match at night
soon may grasp the torch of liberty.
While a dog tail dipped into a wound
holds the mirror union of the senses.

And all in war of space and time,
I dream to drink with you
from the fountain of strength, and wait
for an unbelievable date to the movies.

Or isn't there a job for you in space
Catherine, with your metal sandwich?
Let's keep the conversation hermetic,
for soon even midnight will be plastic.

I will forget the ads I read
in this Mechanics Illustrated:

"Be a locksmith" and fumble for lost keys
of paradise. I have my own shop now.

Ah, to the movies, where you hero in
black sulphur spurs dives in a wedding of
    mustangs
(An eagle collects doorknobs in the
    afternoon,
  the code: In Honor of Autumn.)

Do those who cannot see, love darkness?
Does nightingale trade its song for fame?
Are you in human form, calm once more
With your imploding love to blame?

Would you run among sweet wild flowers
To warn of Autumn in ominous tone?
I ask the generation with a hardening smile
If killing goes will love be all alone?

If destiny could be bought for latest kicks
Could I sell a man screaming in an hourglass?
Could I sell my pin-up queen for charity?
Tell me, my burning rose, all about this.
Tell me in words I cannot understand,
Because if I do, I will cry to hear
Myself above all others,
And crush you in fabulous evening.
Then go to my room and rinse my hair in
Cream rinse and think of pill-day Cadillacs
With continental spares and chrome rear
    ends,
Undercoatings of violent lace.

And read Kustom Kar magazines far into the

night...
Dreams of billfolds full of money,
Nightmares of conspiracies.
Is this the head I'm stuck with
Born to an age which makes me thirty?

Or I may see a laborer in the sun
Who dreamed he was a poet
And wandered over a hill to a shining city
Where he peeks into the final version of
    himself.
And remembers the love songs of warm-
    bosomed singers
As in the days of dying and rebirth,
Melting in a wilderness of armor
Trembling in fear when doors flew open.
When poet ran around the globe
Collecting love and rage and tongue,
Anointed with hair oil
Infiltrating the last detail of the universe
Gold coins pouring down the street.
(Before you ran up your hill in ecstasy,
Removed from ghettoes of clamoring style)
Asleep in dawn tail fissures
The boy dreams of nights in K.C.
Jr. gangsters, jazz, and Mr. B collars,
Chuck Berry, Bill Haley, and Elvis singing.

I'm over here, of course,
melting in war stories,
playing a sweet mournful tune
on a hollow flute made from
the bones of dead junkies.
I'm singing the Great Speckle Bird
under the street lights in N.Y.C.

Now I am here, staring out a window,
people moving about
trying to tell each other something,
put your raincoat on do you want to go next
how long since I saw you
and got that old feeling?
I can hear Chet Baker singing,
I get along without you
well, except when leaves …
Yeah, that's total recall.
Can we go somewhere and talk
through the ether?
Remember, the shack on North Main,
night in December soft rain and fog
I had death throes in my hands
and every road of life closed down.
And you trying to help me
and not go under yourself.
Sick lightening in a far off storm.
Followed the road of those before me to the
      West.
(Harlow with your name in silk.)


Tonight I ride in the
beautiful mountains
in a ragged chartreuse Ford,
under the moon with heaven close
to earth of winding road and sounds of
cymbals and chants and songs like
Wildflower and Moon Over Alabama.
Julio chuckling privately
at moo cows in the pasture,
moon on the dashboard
like a flower…
Creator, Destroyer, Preserver.

Do not tell the stars
I sing like a traitor
From radio Apocalypse Rose.
Is there something I can say to you
O Radar Queen in Compton's Cafeteria,
Before puke and blood melt in the street?
Is there a promise in the bedrooms
Below fixed bayonnets of Paradise?
We are linked by our tongues' wall
With hand grenades on our mouths.
Where were you before a protest was needed?

Could I walk out the door and say,
"Baby I'm gonna get mine."
But without missing too many meals
I can buy a Polaroid for $29.98,
And take pictures of troops and pickets.
Or Mr. Hyde of Cut Corner who wishes his
was black leather. Or 19 year old David,
who burned himself, left a note reading,
Buddhist Monk, Inquire at Fairoaks Street
"I die for all mysterious things."
Or the blind on Market Street
Or the man with no legs,
Perhaps no nearer to panorama than thou.

Would you be cruel
if you spent a life
carrying Venus to Mars
with a light in your head?
While under the bridge of forgotten gold,
Betty throws a wine bottle against the wall.
And a wino was stacked in a bed of
    cardboards

dead for many months smelling.
More cardboards were piled on him
And more winos slept on top on him,
for many months smelling.
When the police dug him out, they said
"He was crushed like a rose in a Bible."

Sometimes flowers bloom in spring
unaware of what the summers bring

From now on
today is the most beautiful,
planters have struck against the ground,
grain is overheard on the melon side of night.
The rose has fainted in the mirror.

Where else can Autumn be?
"I'm over here."
Again?...
But the windmills chopped the sky
Are you still there with spying creators pinned
    to streetlights
Turned on too soon to clairvoyant blue?

Break the mind trap in time stigmata,
Call back the runaway climax from the
speed of Christmas squared. Because
you seem to know too much just beyond
the conversation. So let's walk down
Market St. where your outline changes
in mercury of your flaming youth
under marquees on the meat block
where teen age hustlers cruise.

The rose that summer held — and gave again,

Has grown your form in re-appearing dew,
Preserved the fragrances of that time began
When seeds were drops of love in rose-red
   hue.
But sweet life must nourish on such sorrow
As each dying makes some men blossom
   through
The blood that fell on each new tomorrow
And you saw this as I was watching you.
Under the influence of all your stars,
In mirrors of your galaxies blue,
The hero and his love became your scars
But this rose picked could not be picked anew.
      To measure you and me in full disguise
      I lay beside our rose of paradise.

## PETAL FROM THE ROSE

Baby, break that mind trap in time stigmata
though your outline has gone beyond the
    changes
of the mercury in your flaming youth!

Weary streets of waiting, walking,
under marquees of all night movies
on the meat block
where teen age hustlers cruise.

Market Street
and the moon is full.
We see an old newsreel with the face of
    Dillinger.
"He smiles on the right side of his face,"
You say, "like Bogart."

Voices in the fog
dispelled the blocks
of waves bright lights hung on.

## ANOTHER PETAL FROM THE ROSE

Apocalypse, Rose, Pin-up Queen of coffee-
    tonk cafes,
all the runaway climax from the speed of
Christmas squared ... call it back.

Rose of summer in the re-appearing dew
call through the dove-tail fissures,
call through the ghettoes of clamouring style.

Break the mind trap in time stigmata,
let me kiss those changes of your
outline in the mercury of flaming youth.

Kiss like birds in the fog
through blocks of waves that
bright lights hang on.

## MOSQUITO STREET

And de TEENY-BOPS
de will come,
and de wine
and de sea splash
to de sun spoly oly,
like de deductions from you door.
HANNA/LITTLE EGGS/DREAM GLOBS/
HATS FULL BULBS/PANIC REACTIONS/
SURVIVAL CLUSTERS/BLAM/SHORT
    CIRCUIT/

Red light short cut
after pubic lips open the door.
HURRY UP WITH SOMETHING
I don't claim magic
but the hill was rollin' with Blake
in the a.m.
the car in reverse
orchestra freight train
growin' into town
hip to the crazy plant
long into the key of vision
into the slots of night
without imitations
and survival kits slamming round.

Standing in North Beach
under jet line of star
faces of tourists shuffle
like DC7 without a tain.
Clark Kent flinches behind his glasses
making eternal undercover bid
for a piece of cloud.

Home to the old dilapidated mansion
on Oak St. Where the bald and nutty
landlady treats the artist like royalty,
with memory of elegant years gone by.
House full of junkies, thieves, meth heads,
Acid spreaders, scene tramps ... the pot
    smoke
thick in the winding staircase. And an
occasional long haired wealthy girl
practicing summer one-airmanship down
in the real nitty gritty by candle light.


Next day Kassandra on St.
hasn't been to bed for 2000 years.
Her face ran when she burned it in the
    mirror.
Gave up her arms when she was robbed
by the Arabs ... went to the white bastard's
    house
... blond, blue eyes.
Said she from amidst her fragrance
"I just fell off five stories in Chinatown.
with my Roman lover
while the spirit war
was going on in the South.
I tricked this chump
from commercial chicken-shit town ...
black Puerto Rican ... just met the punk,
can't stand him ... drunk Ancient Age ...
I was bruised from head to foot ...
Went to Reno where I was Regina
and the Taurians cleared the street.
Then back to the record shop
where I live on Wednesdays ...
This fuckin' high yellow

he knows voodoo…
and all his fuckin' paintings of
clowns crying, I tore them up…
the Martian burn…he wanted to live
on my pussy, he say, 'get up and wash.'
MUTHERFUCKER, suck it funky!
He wore 8 pairs of pajamas
sucked off my pussy and I bled
all over him…
Ain't that cold?
I burned my ovaries with a sunlamp
up in that room
with tricks from the political convention.
Detectives came up,
say I didn't have enough luggage
…shavin' kit with razor and dope.
Dick Dog Taurus
pulled out his prick
looked like leprosy,
white scaly scabs…
I had to put 5,000 band-aids on.

Found this chick,
she tried to finger fuck me
for the first time…
K Y on the night stand…
all the fags had a key to the kitchen.
Jumped on my lover's chest
with spikes on…he took me to King Tut
exhibition…marks up and down my arm,
from meth crystal palace."

(Mida Vida tattoed on her hip.)

## THE AUTHOR:

Script in hand
Stands revealed in Awesome Splendor.
Adult skull
Arms outflung
As in forgotten time
When night fell…
Shimmering vertebrae
Trapped between hunters and the rim
Green-spaghetti arms
Skeletal needles
Dark cloud of hair
Careful hands.
Grey snake on green path
Trash dump traces
Visitors besiege the writer's window:
Bright eyed
Glass models,
Iridescent pygmies
Marring the vanilla,
Yielded ingredients
For ice cream and tooth paste.
What is it? The grime of centuries
stage for an awesome collapse?
Leaving the small boy in the center wide eyed
     and openmouthed.
To dance, to sing, to play the guitar
Warm glimmer: A new species?

## RAGTIME

The Young are pretty;
Meth & Go Go eyes...different than
the stock exchange? Where they all coming
    from?
is that
the teen-age revolt exploding in the street?
Collection of independent spheres
pushing to the front
in all night beetle post-beat rock an roll,
turning on to secret visions or sugar cubes
dancing in their heads in pre-semester pads
they're prolly not as power hungry as I am
    be-
cause I want it all. But the only trouble
with being like God is that I have to be like
Big Compassion
and that hurts too much
like tenor sax
splitting notes...
Like loosing form, spreading into other's
    worlds.
Besides I'm too paranoid to be president—
or myself, sometimes for that matter.

What am I gonna do next?
It's hard tellin' what I'm gonna do next.
You say I said that
so you would anticipate I'm gonna do
something interesting next?
Yeah, you're right.
All the words came home.
Don't even take dope no more.
Can't bring on those hallucinogenic smiles,

(awareness, wasn't it?)
But those cigarettes are killin' me.
Went down to the corner
to buy myself a drink
I thought it would help me
because I could not think.

A man walks up…
"What's on tonight, Young Blood?"
"Ain't nothin' to it
no one on the set.
Regular meat block routine,
it's a little rawer down here."

Went to my room
thought of a great line,
couldn't find my pen.
Room a mess piled high.
Peter walks in, baffled…
asks if I'm doing spring cleaning.
I live like this.
I'm very lazy,
besides the brain watchers predicted
I would be in the fields by now.
                —*The Tenderloin, San Francisco 1965*

---

## FOOYR BONY ROBOT DRIVER

It's a craztown scepter
old folks round the hard jackpot.
Take the hard edge off
waiting for a shot,
light headed and dizzy,
just like Virus X.

A little high and
a little breakfast then
to put on some gravity.
Just glide around the corners
in overdrive. It's the best
stuff in town. Waiting
on the front row.
No time to be concerned
with any issue.
Cut down your speed
in your own time zone.
Wait for it all to go past.
Same canyons,
same bridges.
Once you get there
in overdrive
and go. That's what I
like about you driver,
you're a boy who notices
things. Shit energy
into the gears. It's a
ying yang conspiracy
in the time trap. An
old Chinese saying.
"For man to follow
woman is evil." Don't
let the three headed
serpent loose under
the moon…O flappy blue.

---

## FOLLOW MY NOSE

Far away in my head
of childhood pantomime,
through the window

caught feigning
of the wheat and honey bee.

Was I in love
when the earth ate the grass
and the sun ate me.
When I gathered Indian arrowheads
from around the farm house.
And watched big ants
crawl all day.

And now in later years recall
any two lines at all...

(While between the wine and Mars at
his hand grenade, I taste myself
and hand you the glass.)

---

## BLUE EYES

Ears at attention
Brooding Majesty
Lesson in bargaining
With hope and fear
Mushroom and mosses
Tiny sun machines
Jigsaw puzzle is pieced together:
out steps a flute player,
"Does the wind always blow this way?"
And got the reply,
"No, sometimes it turns around
and blows the other way"
And so on and so on.
Buried the open-pit creatures of the sea.

## POEM TO NADA

Nada, soon to be like a fox.
Nada, your hair I remember.
Nada, I want you to know the radio,
the room where the memory of your face
is pinned in a prism...
Nada the eternal daybreak,
the fairy's vengeance... Pinned in world.
Nada, the ripples in the late April sky,
above the gate swinging, saddened by use.
Nada, we talked to each other,
Making us inhabitants of life.
While the moon grows above flowers
with the promise of morning,
the lengthen the dead
in the late April sky.

---

## JANUARY

When Stars forget their faces,
and a closer look at nature becomes
cruel. Birds fly ashore in April
remembering their eggs in the sky.
Then I click like memory in birth
and death, and see the branch
and stream of law entwine.

The spider weaves haphazardly
forgetting the first part of the
spiral. Tired, perhaps, of the
trembling fly. But when the broken

web of frost becomes the ground
with unknown explorers with internal
sextant and shaky compass lined.
What is unfurled in vendor's empty

wares. What tracks unwind in radar
screen of all events. Lone wolf. A
warm slinking fact in the film of life
around the earth. To cold frost town.

Tracks in the newly fallen snow over
vortex plains, cold twisted trees
gnarled tough in their scale of years.
Scraggly arms that reach for the moon.

As in a month the moon repeats its
fundamental note. Involuntarily stomachs
drift to Venus … she repeats hers, and
within the baby yet another aspect opens.

Hungry wolf cannot see the beginnings of
    snow,
tracks over the mirror in the hungry wind of
    ice.
Secret atoms passed on and on in the
    howling wind.
(Home to unwind the mummy roll by roll?)

Is there a part of me, an edge I
cannot peer beyond, a hidden angle,
a side I cannot see, A ghost? But then?
Your admiration unfolds my face
with a river of peacocks across my brow,
a flutter of light years in my chest.
But what is applause when drama closes?

# MANSIONS

Am I delivered unto these old doors
where keyholes are too large,
and good-bye letters lie askew
under smelly windowpanes?

I heavy step the wino stairs
of phantom murderers,
while an ancient line of ghosts
walk up to my eyes to peep.

And O that breath of sleep
I have at night,
crossing over hills of prairie hay
where early frost stigmata
bears the light.

Like in a western movie
I run in hills
leap over rocks and stones
carved in their time there.

Hiding in crevasses
I drew smoke from outlaw guns,
some fun there, dying on the run.

How I climbed
with my Winchester in my hand,
chasing Einstein, shouting
questions with a Kansas twang.

How like a movie
dreams go,
in which I fell asleep,

awoke after everyone had gone
and tugged my wraps around me
to go home alone.

O thou ancient, lucky warriors,
with your enemy in front of you,
how will thy bow and gun
and arrow fend now,
in a Winchester Manson,
with every window to a subdivision of home.

(Inspired by the Winchester Mystery House
In Santa Clara Co., Calif.)

---

## THE EVENTUAL DEATH OF ANIMALS ON COBALT DEFICIENT PASTURES

Terrible this morning,
I washed the ants down the drain,
so I could eat from my plate.
Warriors rode past in Cadillacs
with flaxen hair on queen bee wing.

Pilots were cool on T.V. brain
scouring the mushroom ghost,
finger phantoms stalking sweet meat joke.
As the reaper takes,
his best gains be.

O crew cut whirligig
in footsteps of dark moon Lilith,
are your faces trapped
in the changes of the drain?

And you, my vogue, my pin-up queen,
my heard freak drama of the freeways,
my virus cup, my morning in December
can you skim across the buss stop
to the windows, or walk in bubbles
of the black boot silence,

These lines are not to chant you,
or sing the music in your motion.
The coffee at the gallery is not
my black commercials, the energy
I shift into the car
is mere suggestion.

No, my sweet woman bursting
in all the years that passed away,
and all the years to come,
will you ever know
what I carry inside me.
And all the art,
and all the drama of the stage,
and all the gala parties
of your kings and queens,
nor inventions new
nor memory transmitted into space
nor all pre-occupation of
your pretty mind
can match, dissolve, or carry it.

## SANTA CRUZ

I feel like a woman uncovered,
Slightly wild, beneath the full moon;
I feel the blush of pastured rose.

I feel the passive moon tonight,
and I am not ashamed,
I want to have love made me,
or to get screwed.

I know the moment of young flesh,
Like the kids turning on to fire down the
    beach,
To be wet with screw,
To me made love to, till shadows ignite each.

Oh! Yes tonight I must build a boardwalk
across the Pacific, with red shoes and
    carnivals on.
Yes tonight while the moon lights Point Sur.

I want a free-for-all where ragtime cells
soar mad with moonbeam skaters,
De-coding wave and spark amd seas,
and energies hang down from pine and star,
fresh, sweet, like Kid Cupid's slim ovaries.

---

## CITY IN THE STATE OF LIGHT

City in state of light
lifetime of related movement,
Why is it in your sewers, the mammal fix?

Must invest in flying fix
must tremble in memories of unseen
     molecules.
Walking to the library I find a book;
In the Physics Library (what)
well I wouldn't expect that from here.
Opened page:
Dear Charley? There is a wheat field here
     and at the edge of it we have our hospital
     (of course it's only a game) there we play
     doctor. (we are five girls) if one of us has a
     pain at the pussy, she goes to the hospital.
     There we have cotton and salves and creams.
                    — *All that have been swiped.*

———

## PG. 133 THE MASS PSYCHOLOGY OF FASCISM — WILLIAM REICH

Oh what messages
as powerful nations tremble.
Joyous supernal they sit on a weed.
And rattlesnakes hidden in the faults
of my wild Wichitas,
my new Ulysses on the Cimmaron
ARAPAHOES OF NO BOUNDARIES
O LUST OF PRAIRIES SUPRESSED
O COPPER Kingdom
Flame of iron hardened
more authority seen
not laced
but bolted to the hands of blood. What does a
     bullet mean
in terms of your own cock. Why bullets at all?
And flesh here

and here unseen in sky
breastplates of armor clash
the silent dance of combat
circling in the clouds
like the ghost of this plow
far beyond the pale human heads
seething from the dust
to chanting clairvoyant passage
dust beside the lightning at the edge of field.
That's all you have
AN ANCIENT SURGERY
like somewhere in romantic vial
the hidden bride
sunken like a catalyst on a sugar cube
while in your bureaucracy maggot eat your
    brain
The groom sprayed into your hair.
Overcome with feeling, a boy with a hatful of
    bulbs
converging zone time and Civil time.
NATIONS BEWARE
Simple for him; declining physical energy
frozen in eternal presence
heat trips mechanism  ghost air unseen
    unfelt
releases his dilemma of reality
he points his finger at his playmate
and simply says, "BANG"
you're dead.

---

## ERASE

The mushroom bombs are in the image
of the mushrooms in the garden

they are dark and damp and gravely.
And I have a madness leaking from my head
like the fruit that lingered too
long in the garden.
O give me sweet air
a bird flying into my nose
cashing its wings behind my eyes
to woo from sleep, the defects of kingdoms,
the vision that break my glands.
Take your bombs,
strangled by the absolute sphere.
I turned homeward, upward to the
    telegraphic sun.
So do not give me your sweet air
no more gives/no one to give/no cries
just crushed tongue
lapping up the spirit of decay
No No do not consider me/erase me like the
    silence
the lie oozes from the sutures
and the song has all been spilled.

---

## CRYBABY DEMONS

Came she from the dark fires burning
in nests of butterflies trembling,
and like a bird
strapped the dark womb upon me
I was trapped like bells in combat
into the beautiful
three-faced mask forbidden.
Oh how that vain store of torture
burned true to the ear and heart of atoms

Like crybaby demons
we are broken in the melancholy handshake
Driven by the guns

———

## THE DAY OF THE COYOTE

I dissolve
but no more in shadow
than into the spirit of the star
which carries my death
directly behind me now,
But it does not carry your killings
and I will carry your hell no longer.
I've eaten a thing called death a thousand
    times for you,
you were powerful
and told you had reason to kill

If you destroy you must create
for lifetimes beyond your comprehension,
and be stuck in a world
of its own time and hell
while others wait.

Watch you pitifully try to capture my time
as you force me to your sewers
and the new buildings circling your towns
living on the rotted deaths of your systems.
During W.W. II, I stood beside a
 B 17 that crashed
and the pilot (I think his name was "Yank")
used the term "blivot"
which in later years was to have cosmic
    implications.

All must feed death
every moment a payment of energy
I measure as I sit here
facing another moment
to fit plans together
that I move toward something
to preserve my being
not yours,
same as when you killed
with primitive weapons
To function from used parts
like a humanor a shadow that once was
a pattern
an endless square dance
caller re-playing words from mouths.
My mouth because I've been the hanged man
and there is no reason to cover you for any
    longer
only to be degraded or a victim of your
    machine
For your sake
do not look in my eyes
or expect me to speak
to put words together
to prove you're alive

You know your intricate electronic machinery
which has formed itself
and holds to an absolute paradox
to keep together
to justify to preserve
itself above all else
and its reasons for sanity.
Stop talking with expectation
witness your own reality

what time, place, thought you're in
I'm on time and not nice again
when you break your law
and drag me to your car
because my hex is longer than your
    calculations.
You are a formula in time
which will appear in a pattern
of unknown will
as equation you will have no more
but to deteriorate in loss of energy
you may call evolution.
Compress that into war
or think me backward
when I read your pitiful face
in uniform and ease your threat
BUT NO MORE
IT'S YOUR ORDER: TAKE IT
or stop this pattern of no meaning
but to re-appear a slow cyclone
of your lifeless roses
Count your steps into
the fake system of your morning class
Or put your uniform on tight
to hold you together
in grenades I cannot throw
into the sewers of your suffering.
Zoo liquid from your blathering
will not cause the reaper or raper to burst
from the temples of your pump
The rat and coyote gnaw
from sewers of your society
they are not tired of these worlds
because they do not speak them
but understand the words you compromised

to build the sewer.
And like the zoo heart
death will peer over your shoulder
like a misguided spectacle
And coyotes hung from fence posts in Kansas
will feel a moist in their dry mouths
I speak for them
hanging with their ears cut off
with leg through knotted tendon braided
If they serve as warning to others
then I say warning
brother unto brother
When it is the day of the coyote
I will weep no harder
nor laugh louder
nor die more
nor speak clearer.
(The word "blivot" meaning:
 trying to put five pounds
of shit in a four pound bag)

---

## DECEMBER
(Wichita, Kans.)

Awkward, standing near soiled anklets of
      death,
money in congress for personal rain of
      arrows,
shot into the eye of pyramids and shackled
      birds
and whitetailed deer cradled in jet stream.

Guilty as homemade sin. Old Injun. Ugh!
      Why me?

Here again? C'mon baby, let's run down to the
river. Let your boobie relays just glide past
the sparks of hellish millions that can't buy,

place we gathered ferns in lighter years
tickling the blood veins of your temples
somewhere in Kansas through the stars to
difficulty. By wandering trees stripped cold.

Mother old and stooped in the kitchen
at 5 a.m. preparing for work. Her old
tough pioneer hands explaining coils
assembled at her minimum wage job.

She who plowed with the John Deere tractor
when I was a babe in a wooden box on its
floorboard, watching the huge tired pull
across the prairie. Smelling fresh earth

turning in sudden spell of wonder.
    Unconscious
king of renewal opened for the wheat seed.
The pop pop of the two cylinders pinging
into the magnetic singing of space.

High to the poles of earth where birds fly out.
Messengers from the inner sun. Who will
    pray
in the silent vertigo of light and speed?
Who can gaze into trees without seeing a
    pattern?

She, now, grievous, worried, shaking her
    head
… as a swimmer tossing water from his hair.

Worried about my alcoholic sister, in jail,
or somewhere in Mission Dist., San
  Francisco.

A rough bar, perhaps, on Valencia St.
where broken Indians fight vague battles.
Her thoughts lost in worry like her
car keys. "Now where did I put them?"

Jehovah's Witness at the door. Pentecost
on the telephone. Billy Graham on the radio.
"Who," as they say in gambling circles,
"really had the nuts on the tables?"

Christmas conjoined on the personality
cross, stuck in the mystic kingdom of self.
The streets swell in holiday bulbs inside
a floating world of bubbles and goods.

A carnival of alchemy in the snow
early frost stigmata on the hay.
Roots in the center of black earth
where Indians begged for food.

... Passed my old house remembering
impossible dances out the door
onto the grass holding pages of
wild poetry I could not understand.

Beautiful and tragic wing of youth.
And now a hollow feeling, north, like
winter white water. A rendezvous in inner
space. Mike says home is where the hurt is.

Where then? Would go east again to
spring blue wood, or south to red
summer fire. Or complete the cross
west again to autumn yellow gold.

---

# DRUG DRAG

Oh ruinous grave of life that did not open,
Flower of the sun that did not bud.
The wild self show
that filled towering balconies,
in vacant houses, unlit barns
and river banks,
while mushrooms languished under
script and key.

Ruins in the hills much like ruins in man,
eroding circumstances,
leaving what part bare,
exposed to heaven in one short life?

Growth of brain is long of day and
towns are far away,
Decaying then when the road is short
and speed has brought much dust.

Though Shakespeare quipped in passing:

"If it be pois'd, tis the lesser sinne
That mine eye loves it and doth first
    beginne."

Could have been about a lot of things.

## TO A DEAD PIGEON:
## UNDER THE FREEWAYS

Dead pigeon lying in the street,
with your ingrown tongue so stringy,
I don't have to stop here and look
at you,
knowing that I have to write a poem
for you,
and worse of all, only caring halfway
that you lie there in final arabesque,

You look like a bird pattern in a rug
only one dimension to the street.
An Eagle you are, I've seen on Indian stone,
you no longer go with choo-choo neck
and spaceman eyes.
You are beautiful there, my beloved flyer,
who merely sought the crumbs of life.
And could some jealous sniper with
and ugly grin have felled you?
Ah well, he only walked here.

But your form on the pavement will
soon go away,
first the feathers blue and grey
and your pinions crushed.
Your delicate ribs.
And you say, "who should want my feathers."

It's not the feathers but the flying...
you see, caught in
physics! astronomy! oh that notions
could line on a scale
But no, I look at you
you free you from my eyes.
With dumb coward glaze
begging voices from the wind you flew.

Myself wanting Venus and Mars
to crush into the dirt we die in,
closing the pyramid of light.
Oh long thin rotting muscles
that once breathed the secrets
of the family bird,
I want to give you ritual
but I'm afraid,
afraid as walking past the blind with tin
cups.
Afraid I cannot pull out.
Afraid there is not reason long enough
to find my way home...
under the freeways.

# TEAR LUST

Crying, with my head on a booth
in the musk of honky-tonk lights,
Falling through a bottomless glass.

Then a long decayed delinquent gaze
into prototype zoo liquid figures
On the dance floor
in the Okie's Bar. My
ears full always
of a phantom voice.
The deep unsung moment of total life
My pockets full of phantom reward.

What if
the mason knew how many groping
hands caressed his wall,
the carpenter how many times
his table held a brow.

How then the preacher knows how many
times I married you in phantom space.

Looking through the vague orange light
I saw a dancer's boot
while the hillbilly singer sang:

"Pick me up on your way down."

And I seemed to remember a note of
metaphysical importance about an Indian
    bear.

And then to the telephone,
passed the vertigo of astronauts
for someone in a generation long ago.

Putting pieces together
as if no other in the world
for at least three minutes.

Then why call?
We could not see into the functions of
    October,
Nor like trees that cannot bear their good-
    bye leaves,

We could not talk.

———※———

# THE LAST OF
# THE MOCCASINS

## THE LAST OF THE MOCCASINS

I was wide awake very early that grey Sunday dawn in SF, and that was unusual. It had been one of those restless nights like what happens sometimes when certain unseen, unnamed conjunctions in the higher cosmos are active. I felt restless like I had been on speed. There were roaches lying around; a hash pipe lay on the old ornate Victorian mantle piece. The apartment creaked and moaned as if the woodwork had absorbed too many vibrations through the years. It had been through the great earthquake and since had been the shelter for beats, poets, writers, painters, filmmakers, junkies, sneak thieves. Its woodwork contained all. The rooms emitted sanctimoniously stained sunrays like in a church or opium den or in a palace of the fixed with the revelations of writers superimposed on dusty curtains.

I had thought of Betty once or twice during the night, not that that was unusual. I thought of her now and then, if she was sober, what were her latest projects. I was thinking about her around 3 a.m. that morning. Had I called her then, it might have made all the difference in the world. That has always puzzled me, little insignificant things, trivial events that could direct a whole change in the tapestry of life. Betty knew this too but she didn't give a damn about puzzling over it. I used to go with her to Reno and when she threw the dice she just didn't care. If she threw ace/deuce or 21 at black jack; same thing. She even got one of the slot machines stuck at Harrah's and it kept going without putting any money in it. I loused up the jackpot for her when I took it for a while, but she didn't care, money was money and was to be spent. Life was life. If she was broke, she would hop a freight or catch a truck driver going her way. Broke or flush, drunk or sober, her one will was GO. And she had been on the GO as far back as I could remember. Chance was part of life and chance was one thing she could have of her own, secretly, even when the rotten society that snubbed her tried to corner all chance, she still had hers, and she could go anywhere anytime and do anything she felt like, and by God she was alive and you were well aware of that the first moments you were around her.

There was really no reason to call her at 3 a.m. Either she was on a drunk, or she was sober, and there was nothing anyone could do if she was drunk except listen to her fill many unwritten volumes of experiences she had lived. I would see her anyway around the following midnight when I picked Frank up to go to work down on the docks. I looked out the window into that grey, dull, foggy, bleak, washed out, viral sky of SF Everything looked too familiar. I hated the thought of doing anything at all that day. I had a bitter acid taste in my mouth. And if that wasn't enough, the raw jingle of the telephone clanged through the grey. Frank called and said Betty had taken some pills around 3 o'clock when she came home from a bar. He tried to revive her and had called an ambulance and would call back. He called back and I heard his words exactly before he spoke them.

Funny thing about death, it operates just like the picture you see of the grim reaper. It severs

shocks or clumps of people from life. Two or
three or more at a time. Judy Garland died that
day. She went out on pills and booze too. Maybe
several unknown people died that day who
were joined together by some invisible bond.
When Huxley died so did Kennedy, Cocteau,
and Piaf, and perhaps more who had something
in common with them, on this earth or in the
cosmos. Betty had some similar traits with Judy
Garland, all along. Maybe that particular part
of the garden of life needed trimming. Maybe
there were others who lived life in the same
way as they, rich or poor, unknown or famous,
it doesn't matter in that respect. It's in the way
you're hooked up to life. The bum goes through
just as much securing his dime as J. P. Getty does
securing his fortune. The reaper trims his own
cosmic garden, if there were too many of this or
that cosmic thread, too much here, not enough
there, disconnected or plucked from this dual
reality, this cosmic thread needed to make the
total weave of existence come out right, or that
with the proper pattern in the proper time and
space, or maybe they were selected with a certain
type life thread to string together molecules and
tie them together in that mirror of anti-matter.
What cosmic thread of anti-matter can produce
life itself, build empires and armies, and string
science far into the planet beads of human
knowledge. This death that feeds on human
life, the fear of it alone pushes humanity along
day by day beyond the event horizon of death
unknown. It just has to be, like Charles Atlas, a
box number in Eternity; it has no overhead, no
cost of operation, it makes life work for it kills

for its pyre, builds altars to it. It severs man's memory in time, contains him, blind, groping in gravity. It rules with fear, keeping predatory beings prowling the dark abyss of time; it keeps man feeding it with his fellow men to satisfy this prince of anti-matter until man can duplicate himself through science. This is all the predatory being can do, his only way out. The worm unlocks itself but loses the butterfly. That night death trimmed and reaped its psychic fibers, it tapped the spirit that drove the body to give to that perfect garden of eternity. The spirit lives through the whole process and Betty's spirit was to be thrown out over the Pacific in symbolic ashes from a plane at Half Moon Bay where she had gone one time to take flying lessons to become a bush pilot in Alaska.

We went to Frank and Betty's apartment in the Indian section right off skid row. As we approached, we saw the meat wagon and police car and attendants and, as in the stark reality of an Ernst painting, two or three grizzly housewives, ghoulish, jovial, and sweaty in their dirty aprons waited for the main performance. I went up and saw Betty lying on her side. That big frame of violent action now still; that overbearing devastating personality which made one cower immediately had stopped, her face and body still bruised by vague drunken Indian battles in the bars. She passed for Indian and fought with Indians over some desperate, suppressed right to live, right to roam, and right to battle. On her table was a headband, cigarette butts, spilled wine, coffee cups, confused numbers from the stock market, the green sheet of horse racing, bookkeeping records; the typewriter waiting for that raw emotion flowing to the drama in the brain, swelling in wine into accounts forever unrecorded unused and unknown in hearts of drinking buddies, and lovers. Just the other night I was talking to her. Ferp was there and Frank too. She was saying how there weren't many of the old rounders left. How they were a dying breed. Ferp was saying, "Nix, Craken, there's a pigeon on the roof." The old hustlers, con men, madams were a dying breed. "Nix, Craken, there's a weed growing in the garden." I stayed awhile to discuss the funeral arrangements with that "Greek Joint" around the corner that was to handle the affairs, that sent out their long black Mafia cars with old grey haired junky men to take us to the last rites. I prepared a final letter to be read.

Dear Betty,

Just a note — a little late as always. Let's be straight now as always-no bullshit. I could have taken you in more than I did, offered you more help, looking back now, how small a thing, an open door, a night or two longer on the couch, a few more hours yakking, and God knows how I would love to see you now, that obnoxious frame pounding at the door saying, "Chuck, let me in."

While you're smirking, one more thing on the subject of love—(sometimes hard to show among the living)—if you thought for one moment no one cared for you, take a look now at how many souls shaken in tears, their hearts heaving in longing—let that be everlasting proof we loved you.

You were many things to many different souls—a child of God, a daughter, a wife, a lover, a pal, a buddy, a chum.

You taught me this: that everything and everyone has its own beauty precious unto itself- the wild mustang, the outlaw, the bum.

And I'll bet you never knew how many things you taught someone—things slow to evolve, things that can't be seen as lessons. You showed me a life force lived to the fullest, cowering to no one in this stinking society that was so eager to belittle you.

For these attributes I gleaned from you, I lobby now for your eternal freedom— EMANCIPATION—one of your favorite words. Now your reward of infinite space, your spirit hitchhiking over this land you love. No more state lines now. Those truck tires singing down that long highway—they can't pass YOU up.

So I thank you for the part of your life you shared with me, and in my books everyone meets again in a better place. I don't even need to wish you luck now as I did in this rotten world. I know you're O.K. So like I always said—see you next time around.

Your Brother,
Chuck

I called the boss to tell him Frank and I wouldn't be unloading freight tonight then went back to Gough St. to climb the stairs where Betty and Frank had slept off long alcoholic nightmares, where Neal too had slept before he quit his fantastic life down along the railroad tracks in San Miguel de Allende. Glen was on the porch, and I tried to tell him what had happened to Betty but I broke down; he put his arms around me and started crying too. It was the end of that pattern of events that seemed to keep me coming back to SF As far West as we could go. Shelter in that queer old city. Every year or so people I knew would gather, leave again for that range of roadmaps, then return. In Wyoming the last herds of the wild mustangs were rounded up. And Betty had thrown ace/deuce.

California the promised land! For all the people of the Plains California was still gold. High wages and good jobs! Movies! Mountains! Oceans! Deserts! Palm trees! Glamour girls! The stories had built up since The Grapes of Wrath and were still building up. Everyone wanted to pack up and go. My first trip there was in the back of a '36 International truck. A binder. And it was still nearly new. We left the farm and put all our belongings in the back of the truck. The tires hummed that long and lonely forlorn flat harmonica blues that always accompanies a trip; the sadness of what was left behind and the hope of the future on that narrow little blacktop cutting through the great Rockies and the red dirt of New Mexico where Indians stood along the road. I remember seeing a man wearing two big hats in Texas. That was very funny. The sunflowers along the side of the road through the Great Plains tipped their heads to the morning sun as if to welcome the shiny red truck. They followed the sun across the sky pointing to that land of challenge of hope and wealth, their heads dotting yellow in the sunset's purple sage under the rainbows going west. The whole mirage of California was ready to loom up in the distance— the sweet ozone of life to fill the nostrils before the rain and in years to come; before the rain and years washed the hope away into the sea that crept at the edge always, always with its eager tongue to lap up the lonely people of the night.

In the back of the truck the children chanted and cheered strange child songs:

Votcha Peecha

Votcha Peecha

Votcha Peecha Voo

Hip, hip, hooray! The dogs are coming!

There, nestled among belongings under the tarp of that wheat truck, the children were having a great time. No worry, no care—that all took place up in the cab. They had a whole truck bed to themselves and a whole vast fantastic world to see. What fun. They went past Superstition Mountain in Arizona where all who went in were to disappear forever!

You mean they would all disappear?

What if a whole bunch of men with GUNS went in?

They would all vanish.

A HUNDRED men?

They would vanish too.

A THOUSAND men?

It would get them all, and they wouldn't come out.

All the men in the world?

They would vanish as quick as they would go in.

This was indeed a very mysterious mountain,

and we should be very careful when we went past it. The fascination lasted several miles and several years. Later I read articles of prospectors disappearing there.

Boulder Dam which later became Hoover Dam was being constructed. Or at least there were dump trucks way down at the bottom, and because they looked so small I thought they were toys and asked if I could have one. We went on to Yucaipa, California which meant "Green Valley" in Indian. We lived in a small stucco house near some orange groves and a little wash. A red snake crawled across the road. One time a visitor came and some of us said he was Bing Crosby's brother Bob. Another said he couldn't be because he had the wrong color socks on. We had a basement school where my older sisters taught me to read. There was a very mysterious basement next door that had gunny sacks hanging from the beams. Of course, there were bodies in them so it was a very scary ordeal to go over there and peek in the basement windows.

I read my first book. It was about a family who found an old boxcar and set up housekeeping. Each bowl, each spoon, each potato was a triumph; a great sign of things going good. Other than seeing some of the boxcars lined up along the roads near small towns where Mexican railroad workers, (the warm fires and the rich browns and reds and yellows of old boxcars, the guitars playing under the stars with faint smell of weed, oh brother gypsy, tortillas dry and white like the parched desert, peppers, peppers hot as that sun in Yuma where I shared tortillas with some wetbacks) and other than remembering eating cactus apples, fried, like the Indians used to.

I didn't really live in a boxcar but it was much the same as when I would find Betty and Frank; it seemed all of us were always starting over again in some cheap hotel. And Frank would come home beaming as he told of his finds for the day which varied from odd jobs with little old ladies to passing handbills or the schedule of feeding down at St. Anthony's Dining Hall or where the nearest good cafe or store was. And Betty would "hit Sally's" (the Salvation Army) for a few bowls and forks and knives. You'd know she was sober then and wanting to straighten up. The danger signals were when she would buy too many pairs of shoes. Most of the really terrible bad scenes happened when she had too many shoes in her closet. She had thirty-three pairs when she died. I played that number in Reno for her and it did pay some. Someone found a good coffee pot. Coffee in crummy little hotel rooms was better than you'd expect. There was something special about it. The boxcar family, cheap cabin camps, hotels and crummy apartments all over the western half of these Goddamn Fucking United States. There was something elemental in life. Barbitol Bob was later to use the term "elemental politics" in warlock Big Sur. The constant chore of the poor: another dime, another cup of coffee, another room, sometimes a window to stare out of, but most of the time little rooms stuck deep inside the buildings. Maybe a story in Betty's memory about bumming around the South with some clairvoyant junky; she threw her coat in the Rio Grande. She was the first born. Left home

early. With a non-refundable bus ticket. Past the
dance hall in Holcomb, Kansas. To Garden City,
Denver. Wildflower. The sunflower of that great
day of the plains which turns its head to the sun
in the morning and follows it across the sky. The
pot of gold ahead. Always the same distance as
if it were attached to a pole in front of you. Like
the greyhounds and the rabbit. Betty won on the
hounds up in Portland once. $200 she said. Or was
that Denver? The truck tires sang and the diesel
whined and the smoke blew into the night. They
had it wound tight pulling that grade to Denver
and Denver shaking high in the mountains like
a mirage in the Arabian Nights. The windshield
wipers wiped away the drops. Clear for awhile,
then blurred. Oh the new life! Find a job get a
room. Denver, the transient city. The immense
mountains and the splendor and the neon lights
of wino visions all ran together. The wipers wipe
the windshield clean. Splattered against huge
municipality buildings, the sidewalk, falling on
the sidewalk, blood running out, to get beat up by
the sadistic cops. One more gash from the same
old morality stick. Time to wipe it clean again,
the windshields blurred, can't see the signs.
Reminder that we aren't really human after all,
we're predatory beasts she'd say. Devouring,
roaming beasts, in the jungle of coffee-tonk
cafes. The jingle of the coins in the pay phone.
"Some of them call to the old folks for dough,
and that's their ace in the hole. Some got girls
on the old tenderloin, and that's their ace in the
hole." The enormous neon call. All searching for
prey. The businessman, the sheriff, the preacher,
away from their wives, away from their towns:

in the doorway below the red neon stands the
salesman with his hard-on, the slimy politician
with his slimy money, the black pimp beside his
Cadillac.  None were emancipated. Wanna trick
mister? Wanna date? How much can you spend?
None were emancipated.  How about around the
world? You here with the convention? Let me
blow you, honey. Perhaps she was the champion
of equity.  Of morality.  Of honesty.  She couldn't
see some dumb bitch just giving it away like a
sucker, taken for everything she had.  Or to get
hung up with a marriage license just to get a
piece of ass.  Might as well get off your ass and
use it for something besides sitting on, honey.
You can't use it up.  Give them a blow job, though,
save your pussy as much as you can.  Love has
nothing to do with it.  Save love for your old man.
Love is living.  Fucking is economics.  Whether
you're sucking someone's cock for favors in that
office building or sucking it down here in the
doorway, it's all the same.  You use your cunt
and mouth to try to latch on to anything that will
make you secure, whether it be a rich man or a
hard cock, right here in the back of this cab is
where love and economics meet. Fuck you, punk.
I don't need you.  Get your fucking rocks off and
get out of here.  I got money, and a place to stay.
My room rent is paid up.  You got a few bucks
to pay my rent? For a night,  hell no sucker, I
want my fucking room paid for a MONTH. I don't
want to worry about rent. (Another shot of booze
and another lesson in why too much booze will
ruin any profession; even the oldest.) Hell no, I
want my room rent paid up.  I don't want to get
caught out on the street.  Everything was lived

up right then. If you were flush you'd spend your money. If you were broke you'd scuffle. Life's little monetary rewards tossed away like an old tissue. Ordinary women do not grasp the meaning: Why labor and wait a lifetime for something you can get tonight? Collect for that long lost love as you go fucking around, chippy. Why not get paid for it instead of chippying around with some punk? Use that pussy, baby, that dollar buys an ounce of raw flesh to feed the hungry desire. That trick popped his nuts before he got it in. Tha fuckin jerk.

The farm was gone now. Where the cyclone funnel clouds dipped down to the ground like a dark anteater making the whole sky black. Right in the middle of day the monster sounded its fury and sent purple orange messages out of the horizon; flashing dark ominous clouds gathered and rolled toward the farmhouses. Tiny people ran into the cellar which was full of spiders and mason jars. A twister! The thunder bellowed as the whole sky trembled and shook. A crack so loud you could feel it. Lightning lit the sky. A zigzag crazy streak, the world was a flashbulb, a picture of everything recorded in a blink of the eye. Horses knew a storm was comin', they smelled it in the air and started to get spooked. It was time to come in from the fields. The ozone ricocheted off the dark folds of eternity. The spider, the horse, the human plugged into special electricity that indicated God was near. Things sped together, stalked out their atoms, demanded harmony, cursed the world, attacked the elements! Shouted and raved at the universe!

Day break, the extraordinary calm in the sky. Parts of the roof were blown all over the yard. Tree branches were lying on the ground, sometimes trees. Time to hook up the plow to the John Deere. To start the compression, Dad had to turn a big wheel on the side of the tractor. It would cough, sputter, and belch. Dad would cuss it, throw down his hat, kick it. If that poor tractor was made out of anything less than iron it wouldn't have had a chance. Bang! Bang! Pop! Pop! the tractor started. The plow turned and the smell of fresh soil gave me a great exhilarating joy. In the pasture the new born calf kicked up its legs. Everything wants to live and expresses it… said my father, gazing out over the cattle. I have always found it difficult to eat veal. Sometimes I would sit in the cab of the International truck and listen to the winds play their vast, forlorn, undying song; while the plow and tractor quivered in a mirage at the horizon. I could barely hear the ping-ping of the two cylinders shriveling into space. At the end of the day the tractor coughed, gasped, lurched, and bellowed as its big iron engine cooled down and died. It panted, kept running and gasping in spasms. And, of course, the freshly beheaded chicken ran insanely through the yard splattering blood everywhere. The wheat was green then golden for endless miles bordered by patches of sod, buffalo grass, a ruined sod hut, old flint arrowheads in the dust.

Betty would come and go in those years. The great war drew near. We kids helped gather scrap iron for the war effort. There were some Mennonites down the road who wouldn't give any scrap iron for the war. I remember later a discussion about the war brought on by the picture of the Statue of Liberty in an ashtray. Something like, they come ever so often, it has always been that way, I would be just the right age for the next one. I was but I didn't go. I did go to a military school in San Antonio, Texas, though. I did think there was a time when soldiering was a great profession. An almost honorable profession if you can say it's the only way to keep the peace. A dedicated soldier fights for the cause of peace. (Like Mac.) There was a time when that paradox was not obvious and there were some brilliant, dedicated romantic soldiers who operated precisely on the premise of fighting to win peace. I liked MacArthur and I liked military school. I was, however, born into the wrong age for an honorable war and I was very clear about that point. I felt I was right even if it seemed the world was wrong. I declared that those who could not see the fallacy of fighting were, in my eyes, insane and by that very declaration made myself insane. Besides I knew more than the generals about the war. I knew already that the whole concept of war had to change to fit the idea of the bomb. I have lived to see that very many are enlightened human beings after all. Now I see them from my window coming back from D.C. The sleeping bags, flags and armbands, thumbing a ride: Brooklyn, Philly; the cold wind blows.

It was almost twenty-seven years ago when that B17 crashed near our house in Ulysses, Kansas. That was probably the most exciting thing that ever happened there. The pilots brought it to a belly landing. They came over to the house and my sisters fixed them something to eat. They gave me insignias to add to my jacket. I was very proud of the collection I had sewn on it. One thing for sure, those guys were heroes. They had enough war stories to fill my mind with vivid pictures of what happened when battleships were torpedoed and airplanes were dogfighting in the air. Betty came home with her first husband around that time. He was a master sergeant who had served a good fifteen years in the army. He told of some of his missions in China. He was a career man who found a home with the army after the first World War. He wrote poetry and said he was related to the writer, Hawthorne. He had incredible stories of the fighting he had done. As a boy, too young for action, I thrived on these war stories. I remember the pictures of the Normandy on fire, of MacArthur, of "Remember Pearl Harbor" pasted on trains and buildings. I had the idea of becoming a professional soldier when I went off to military school in San Antonio. I think it was a good place and I kind of liked the idea of soldiering. I was a very good student, though I was very lonely on those warm, balmy southern nights. I used to go sit out by the road, and kind of weep down inside. I wanted something. I stuck it out my freshman year.

I missed the Cavalry with the formation of horses jumping hurdles; a rider standing on their backs, around the parade grounds, the yellow patch on the jacket, the kids in my barracks, the meanest. Most of them were older upper classmen. We hid whisky bottles under the floor and stuck burning brooms in the faces of unwary sleepers, unscrewed the water faucets, fought, tortured the weaker boys. After my freshman year I dropped out of school. I was given a '51 Chevrolet which I immediately ruined by turning it into a hotrod, I split the manifold and put dual pipes on it. I lowered it and leaded it in. It was a brand-new car and I ruined it and kept trading it in on older junkier cars. This was because I wanted a hotrod.

I went to Yuma, Arizona, around El Centro, California Drove over to Mexicali a lot. Took girls out to the sand dunes between Yuma and El Centro. Just like the movies with whole waves of shifting sand. There was a wooden road through there from olden days. I drove over to L.A. with my dual pipes roaring. I had a duck's ass haircut which was to become popular in the Elvis era. I wore my shirt collar turned up and my Levis very low with the bottoms of the cuffs turned inside to look tailored. Maybe a chain around my neck, motorcycle boots. That was the costume of the day. I made a trip or two back to Wichita, left again for California in my Olds 88 convertible. Drove back to Quartzsite, Arizona and hired on a pipeline. That was a very rough and dangerous job. I saw a Caterpillar with a side boom crawl right up on top of the inspector's car on the right-a-way and went right on. We were lowering in the pipe which had to be done early in the morning while it was still cool; otherwise it might expand and jump off the skids for miles ahead where the welders were working. Which it did and caught someone between the pipe and a half-track. Another accident happened when the butane stove inside the gang truck blew up. I followed the pipeline up to Flagstaff and Kingman, Arizona. I traded a new GMC pickup my Dad had given me in on a big Roadmaster Buick. I had a young brunette and a cute redhead in Kingman. I was getting lots of young high school pussy. They would come over to the cabin I rented and stay with me. I was driving my Buick around and going to work before dawn and quitting after dark. I would drive a winch truck or a Cat or help "swamping." I used to sing "Don't let the stars get in your eyes/too many days/ too many nights to be alone/ If love blooms at night/ in daylight it dies/ don't let the stars get in your eyes." It was hard to leave those sweet little girls, but I had to roam. I "drug up" and threw my grip in the car and took off for the Northwest to Oregon where Betty lived. Gunned it to ninety, a hundred miles an hour toward Las Vegas, across Boulder Dam again. This time it didn't look all that big. I was clipping along toward Reno in that very dark Nevada sky where there ain't light one out across the land. I was the only thing in that darkness. The only light was a timid star or two and my headlights. No farms, no houses, no sign of nothing. I turned on the radio and the newscast was about the mysterious Abominable Snowman. I started looking behind me, looked into the back seat of the car, pressed the gas a little more. Hit a snowstorm in the mountains pulled into Reno late that night. I was too young to gamble, so I rented a big luxury room in the Hotel Mapes. The smell of the leather car seat and the perfumes and the pussy lingered in my brain. The lipstick, the crisp wind blowing the silken hair. Smooching, the first hot kiss when the tongue feels around inside another's mouth. The whole ritual of entry being discussed with tongue around tongue. The breasts perked up and in my mouth, my tongue wrestling with the nipple. Then my hands down into the warm jeans pressing on the soft juicy hair. My finger down into the warm perfumed box. The jeans peeled down and the tongue sunk as far as it would go. The bed was real nice but I couldn't stay in it all by myself. I found the bellman and slipped him a fin and asked him what he could do about getting me a girl. I let him see a hundred dollar bill as I pulled my wallet out. A little later a nice blonde appeared at the door. Or at least peroxide, since her pussy hairs were brown. She was O.K., and besides I was never very particular. They didn't have to be that slick five and dime store beauty for me. Sometimes I liked to fuck their personalities too. That is I liked them as people and tried to get to know them. I used to have erotic fantasies with my sisters' cutout dolls and coins. I would pretend I was buying some pussy. She was very professional and her hobby was painting she told me as she bathed my prick and checked it for the clap. What do you want to do? Oh I don't know. She started going down on me while I got into a trance over such an object of desire. Professionals always use their mouths when they can and save their pussies. Besides then the prick is hard and wet and ready to come by the time she puts it in. I started eating her pussy; she said that usually costs extra but she liked me and would let me do it. I buried my face in her snatch, that sweet tormenting snatch that fed my hunger and buried my anguish and anxiety though her passion was counterfeit and my money wasn't; still I suppose to some the element of barter interferes with the emotional scene. Not me, she could be my lover, though I never knew her name. How many only love a part of a person anyway. I loved the part that was nice and made me feel good and I didn't mind paying for it if I had the money. She sucked until I came in her mouth and I helped her get dressed slipping on her shoes and gazing hypnotically up her dress far into the dark sea of life, the enchantment hidden in the shadows of her thighs. Pretty soon it would just be in my memory. A subtle fiction that tended my desire, did the job well and vanished with money tucked inside her hose to give to a tough pimp to gamble on the tables. I sank into the starched sheets lonely as that Gideon Bible on the dresser. I took off that day in a snowstorm, spun out on a curve and crashed up my fender, pulled it out enough to continue, rolled into Prineville, Oregon where Betty was living with her second husband, a handsome educated man from New Jersey who owned a lumber mill. A heavy drinker, he, and a good spender. He took Betty and me up to a real nice whorehouse over in Bend, Oregon. There were some dolls there who came out in their trick suits and introduced themselves while we took our pick, he paid for my girl  and she took me back to her room and washed my cock, then started jacking me off. There were mirrors on the wall and ceiling so we could see our bodies at almost any angle.

I ran over a rock in my Buick and ruined the motor. Betty got restless and wanted to go up to

Wyoming and Canada; I said I'd go with her and we took off north. We must have been near Coeur d'Alene, Idaho when we got a motel. Betty was looking great. She was very tall and slim in her slacks. She was wearing a light leather deerskin jacket with the longest fringes I had ever seen. She said she was ready for anything and anyone. We went on up toward Kalispell, Montana, along a route Betty had previously worked sometime ago. The snow and wind was blowing and her little '49 Pontiac convertible hummed right along. She could go through a town the first time and spot where the action was. She would stop and ask the madam how business was and talk shop for a while and maybe stop and work. She would put me in a hotel downtown and come over to see me in her off hours. She may have known the madam before, or had heard of her through other girls. She would meet new girls who had just turned out, or old ones who knew the racket from one end to the other. Helena. Pocatello. Boise, and back to Prineville. We started up to Canada but didn't have enough money to get in. I supposed the customs agent was a typical Canadian prude who pegged us for being riffraff from the States and he didn't want us in his country with no visible means of support. I stayed around Prineville and went to work on a rock crusher that crushed up rock dynamited from the mountains. Betty and her husband lived on good scotch and when they and their friends were drinking anything could happen. I remember we were up in another small town where a lumber grader lived. A good lumber grader could make an extremely high

wage. We went to his house and drank scotch (he
spent all his money on it) and Betty said we all
blacked out at once. All I remember was seeing
one member of the party in the basement of the
Moose Lodge playing cards, and another at a bar,
I saw Betty pulling down her pants right on Main
St. The sheriff came up and she asked why he
wasn't out catching robbers. They stayed drunk
most of the time. I found a girl who kept wanting
me to say I loved her all the time. I followed the
rock crusher plant over to Crater Lake, Oregon,
and worked there for a while then headed back
to Wichita.

I drove back across Nevada, again out there
alone in the night. This time, sure as hell I saw
'em. I knew it would be just a matter of time.
I knew I was going to see the damn things. A
sudden chill crept over me. I slowed down the
car and wondered what to do next. I took a deep
breath. The panic was over. I thought what the
hell, what can happen, maybe I should just keep
calm and try to make contact, like in stories or
movies. After I decided I wasn't afraid and I
started to become interested, they shot off out
of sight. It was just like the accounts I had read.
It appeared right out in front across the sky, a
reddish cigar-shaped thing with what looked
like portholes in its side. And from them came
the traditional saucer objects zooming out.
They were very fast and disappeared rapidly
in the black Nevada sky. I started whistling a
tune and humming a little ditty. What else was
I to do? I drove on through the dark mountains.
I headed up toward South Dakota where I had

worked on our farm as a boy. I had driven all around that country in the late forties with my father who spent most of his time in a car just driving around figuring. He knew every road in the western half of the U.S. He had been over them time and time again since the days he was a trucker during the Depression. He would get in his car and take off for Texas, Dakota, California, as casually as most people would prepare to go on a Sunday drive. I would happen to see him at some people's house in a different state, he would just resume the conversation where we had left off or start talking about the price of land or cattle or whatever. I used to go with him and help drive. He might drive through a whole state without saying a word, or would look out over a herd of cattle or a particularly good piece of land and comment on it. He could look at a herd of beef and tell within an ounce what they would weigh or within a penny how they would sell. He knew land too, every inch of it he knew how good it was, what amount of alkali or acid was in it, what it was worth, how good the crops were on it. It was just like people going window shopping. He would look over every familiar bit of the West. He made and lost a million dollars in cattle and land. He was impatient, always on the go, buying here, selling there on a lark. He sold six sections of wheat land all in one lot in Dakota. Sold the crop on them too, over the telephone, just because he was pissed off over the cold weather. He was always restless and thought of the great high plains as the great high seas he used to sail. A rebel at heart, he would sometimes recall such things as a mate's words concerning politics,

"the likes of you and me, sailor, are just ballast."
Or he would defend Jimmy Hoffa, saying he was
no worse than those God damn politicians taking
bribes. Sometimes he would get philosophical
when the stars were high in a canopy above the
earth. He would say the whole thing is so vast
and huge that whatever or whoever is behind it
all ain't gonna let a little thing like man figure it
out. Anyone who tries to figure it out will just go
mad. Behind each universe there is another —
ours is like a speck of sand on the beach. To even
think about the hugeness, the vastness of it will
make you crazy. Better be gettin' a farm, some
land and start a cowherd. Land is the only real
wealth. If you get a piece of land paid off and call
it your own, nothing can touch you, no matter
what the shape the country's in, you're gonna
be safe, you can grow your own food, your own
beef. Sometimes he would stop the car and walk
a mile or so out in the fields examining the crops
or the soil, he would thrash a wheat head or flax
pod in the palm of his hand to see how ripe it
was. He knew the lay of the land out west better
than most people know their own backyard. Next
he might take off to Australia, South America,
to dream up an empire of land and cattle. He
liked to see grass grow everywhere except under
his feet, and I guess when you were born in No
Man's Land and worked as a boy for a dollar a
day then sailed the seas it would be kinda hard
to just sit down and not dream or plan the next
move. I heard that train whistle pulling that
grade out of Sparks, Nevada, in my memory
when he was a brakeman and took me up in the
engine with the fireman and the engineer and

let me pull that whistle. They gave me an extra brakeman's hat with a badge. I musta been about three years old.

Down to Platte River country on into Wichita. Wichita was still very wild then, and I started taking bennies and going to the Cowboy Inn. Anything went. Men dancing with men. Women dancing with women, gambling, fights, shoot-outs, and even fires. It burned down one day. We used to go out there and score pills from the hillbilly musicians. "Poor old Kawliga," and Hank Williams' voice renewed in my ear from the juke-box in small cowboy town cafes along Montana's cow trail main streets. I saw the Arkansas Traveler in there one night. He had been up for murder once. He's the kind of guy who didn't give a damn and I mean not a damn about nothing and nobody. He came in and put his bottle on a table. He jerked one guy out of the booth and knocked him across the room. A couple of young student type cops came in with crew cuts and horned rimmed glasses and pistols and proceeded to tell him there was a law against having a bottle in the club. (One of those stupid laws about liquor they had in Kansas.) The Traveler said, "Fuck ya punks." Then the two peach fuzz cops made the mistake of telling him he had to go with them. "I ain't goin' nowhere with you punks," he said, as he jerked their guns from their hips. "And next time I'm gonna kill you if you try an' draw on me. No one's gonna scare me, ever, so take these water pistols and shove them up your asses." The cops left embarrassed. It was rough around Wichita for cops. One pulled a guy over and asked him what he was doing out at that hour. The guy pumped the cop full of lead. Bad question, bad answer. I only hope it was one of those sadistic cops from Kansas, Oklahoma, and Texas who beat up Betty on many occasions. Buffalo, the wrestler, was around then, he had a yellow streak in his hair, but not down his back. I saw him in a bar downtown take on the whole basketball team. He knocked several of them over the booths. And the bartender told the basketball team to leave because they were causing trouble. That's how tough Buffalo was. Danny also took on the whole basketball team one time in his motel, but he did it on his back. Wichita was swinging then, crazy in the raw. There were some of the funkiest bars in the world there I'm sure. There were no queens like the mad Wichita screamin' queens, and tough dykes chewing cigars, knocking the hell out of men. There were rough cowboys and cheap hoods, small time Missouri Oklahoma gangsters. The town was wide open, I spent a lot of time in small Spade clubs listening and jiving to such later big names as Chuck Berry, Bo Diddley, Fats Domino. Fats Domino had done some real down home hillbilly-zydeco stuff before he became famous. Jimmy Mammy came by and said, listen here to this, man. We sat for hours listening to Fats Domino singing Don't Leave Me This Way, Please Don't Leave Me, and Rosemary. He came to the Mambo Club and we were there to greet him. He drove up from Louisiana in his old dented Cadillac. What was nice about it then was you could see all the future stars in some little dive on a Saturday night, if you watched the billboards down in Spade town. They came to gig in their own clubs before white people picked up on them. Also some of the jazz musicians had come down from Kansas City after the Norman Granz concerts busted up. There were some good musicians around. Pack Rat the bass player. Sonny, the sax man, pointed to a note on his axe that was rusted over and Sonny said he never knew it was there. Pack Rat ate nose inhalers all the time. We used to get what was called Oxy-Biotic which was a brand of nose drops that would make the present day methedrine seem mild. "Oxy-Biotic will make you neurotic!" Pack Rat plucked his bass and chanted. Scoo bop to do, de bip bip. His eyes rolled back and closed with the look of pleasure (King Pleasure) until the next set. Be de be bop. If I want chop suey I go to St. Louie. To Kansas City like Swwiingging man. He would know people only by their astrological signs. He lived on nose inhalers. Nose inhalers were the source of amphetamine then. He packed his bass fiddle on his back wherever he went. He was always getting evicted because he just let things go to pot around him, things would pile up. Candy wrappers, trash, junk, it was all part of his cosmos. His wife was a junky, man, and like his kid was always dirty and hungry and like Pack Rat took ice cream from the kid and told her it wasn't good for her. He would eat it himself. Not that Pack Rat was really bad it was just, well a thing like, he had to live, man. But he ate so many inhalers he usually wasn't hungry, he just dug doin' his thing and that's all, he would get behind his axe and his playing and groove, he saw people as loaves of bread or Doberman Pinschers, or fuzz or fay, an you wanna smiz zoke a jiz zoint of griz zass. Shuffle Shuffle on down here pops and turn on. I'm high as a cloud, makin' the scene, going on down the street in my Mr. B. collar and my pegged pants and one button roll jumpin' with my friend Sid from the City, and like Sid came up from the city, Symphony Sid his head hid, because he stuck his head in a corner one time in a bust because he thought the cops wouldn't see him then. He was busted for pills, Dr. Gimmy Gommy's Goodies. Me and Phantastic Phil jumped in my brand new '53 Roadmaster and took off to Oklahoma City. We had drunk a whole bottle of Oxy and we was flashing, it went right to the top of the head and felt like the air was little stiff needles dancing on the scalp, little pressure holes that put you in touch, like finally the whole oppressive lid was off and you were movin', movin'. We were swingin', flashin', talkin' man, we felt like super genius, we could talk for days about anything, everything. We felt real friendly, real warm, real nice. I spit out the window of my car and it ran down the side of the door and ate all the paint off in little streaks, I swear to God, man the paint had all peeled off where the spit had been. That Oxy-Biotic was terrible stuff. It was even more powerful than meth. It was quickly taken off the market. I remember going to little backwoods towns and checking their old stock of Oxy. I drove down toward Guymon, Oklahoma, where I had gone in my old Dodge when I was sixteen to join my mother in her Auto Daredevil Show. She drove a car with someone on the hood through a wall of flames. They used to take little '34 Fords and run them off a ramp and sail in the air over a bunch of cars. Now I was driving down these same highways in my Buick. It seemed I was endlessly crossing the same paths, driving down the same highways maybe on pills or pot with the radio blaring from empty space of night from the mad Wolfman (a very esoteric all night disc jockey from ekz ee el oo. This is XELO from Whattis, Chihuahua, Republic de Mexico, 100,000 watts or whatever, strung along fence posts and over mesquite trees just on the other side of the law and the FCC. I went down that same road. One history, keeps going back, down that same road, different intervals, different times I got some Oxy, and some weed, and some Mexican crisscross bennies and went back to Wichita, to these people who really never thought of themselves as any group, it was rawness, and that would have overdone it ever so slightly which would have been too much, but there was a closeness, a family of losers, gypsy-like, musical, apart from the stream of society. And that jive we were putting down had a real special significance because there weren't too many swinging or groovy people then. You had to have some notes to compare. You had to be somewhere and know something about it. You were eager to meet some of your own kind 'cause they was special, it was different then. That same jive talk means nothing now. But then, wow, that was language.

It was a very sad time. The whole town was into mad consumerism just before Christmas. Christ on the cross was always the number one concern in Wichita. The old sand pit down the

river from where I lived as a kid had been turned
into a lake and there was a huge shopping
complex, a whole city out there with thousands
of families in station wagons relieving their war
anxieties, sexual anxieties, god anxieties, or
psychoses, by getting in their station wagons to
hurry and scurry a few blocks in angry traffic to
get inside a store to CONSUME. It seemed like
such a relief to be able to BUY anything, anything
at all whether you needed it or not. Another hot
dog from the stand. Another milkshake. Another
malt. Another pizza from the hut. Another
chicken from the shack. Another taco from the
Tico. There sprung up more carry-outs than I
had seen anywhere.

I called up John and Phil and asked them if we
could get together a little bit tonight because I
was preparing to leave the next day. When I went
in to this 3.2 beer joint out near the U, where they
were already into a conversation about events of
the last twenty years.

–It was right after the old Skidrow Beanery.

–Yeah. I met this old wino on this street. I'd
never walked there in my life. At this time I'm
walking, I have a sack full of Gallo wine. I never
drank wine, but I had this big brown paper sack
full of Gallo wine.

–He been talking all night?

–A while ago I just set him up and just went,
programmed him.

–You programmed me?

–He's got so much of those inhalers in his
system he can't stop now.

–Nixxo verado klacto zzt brrt,  I have a
complete one in my pocket that's never been

used, but these are dexedrine spansules and two biphetamines, black biphetamines, which I acquired early this morning.

–Black biphetamines?

–You know that bedroom, that old bedroom of his? He took me by his house.

–That old bedroom that used to have Debra Padget all over it? Is he still living there?

–She?

–Who?

–Debra Padget.

–No. Debra been gone by the wayside years ago. She was replaced by Jacqueline Kennedy and Superman and uh ...

–He has black paperbacks all over, swastikas ...

–I have TWO books, two books I have, I have The Rise and Fall of the Third Reich, a black paperback which I traded a hardback in perfect condition for, just because the hardback is too heavy to hold when I have to hold my magnifying glass with one hand.

–He disappeared out of the room into the bathroom and did up an inhaler. He got so high he did something like throw a razor blade in the toilet with anger.

–Not with anger, man, with gusto. No, man, with FLAIR.

–I thought you were going to tell us you had found some Oxy-Biotic stuck away somewhere.

–Not even the old wrinkled burnt out boxes that the bottle used to come in. It's gone by the way. It's a thing of the past, that is a piece of memorabilia never to come this way again.

–Remember how we used to get high on Oxy and discuss the profundities and the intricacies

of nature, man, and the Universe? For weeks at
a time.

–I remember one time we started at the
orange juice stand where we had retired to,
repaired to, to dissolve our chemicals in orange
juice so they don't taste so horrible, when we
scarfed. We scarfed, ahh, we smacked our lips,
walked out of the orange juice stand, started our
little traverse, our little trek toward the red and
black MONSTER Buick, a juggernaut in the sky,
sitting on the streets. Charles had forgot where
he parked it, like always, he never forgot, it was
one of those things he used to put on, where'd
I park my car? So we find the car, hmm, hmm,
hmm, we drive, Ronny says, hey man, haaay man,
let me tell you about this chick I met last week
in the park. And from that, from that sentence
man, that story goes from two in the afternoon
to four in the morning and he STILL, I swear to
god, twelve to fourteen hours telling the same
story, hasn't finished yet, still setting the scenes
for every aspect of that story, not what I've been
doing, I'm twice as illiterate, twice as elongated,
and elucidated. Twice as interested.

He thumps the table as he talks.

–You're thumpy. Thumpy tonight.

–Are you going to be Bambi?

Pause.

–What ever happened to your old Cadillac?

–Oh, that's a long story. I left it by the fortune
teller's house.

–Remember that time we drove up to Salinas
to work? You almost burnt your motor out in your
'48 Caddy. You didn't give a shit. You drove right
on, and we went to see New Faces with Eartha

Kitt and thought it was great. We flipped when the guy came out and said BENZEDRINE right on the screen.

–We were living in the Crescent Cabins. Crescent motel early cotton plantation shacks. Tacky beat up cabins with outdoor toilet. Around the cabins were two Cadillacs, formidable to say the least, looking bad around these horrible little run down beatnik shacks we had. Inside we were starving, eating whole dirty rotten potatoes someone had dug up from somebody's garden, man. We sent Terry and the pirates into a store to steal some food and he comes out with a GALLON jar full of mayonnaise. Now what the hell we gonna do with mayonnaise, nothing to put it on. You came in saying we got this job pushing little buggies around. They turned out to be cement buggies weighing about a half ton apiece, impossible to push through the mud and scrap wood and metal. An animal couldn't be expected to do this. You ran yours off the side of the excavation and quit. We started laughing at the absurdity of the scene and couldn't budge them. All except Terry who thought it was time to eat lunch after about a half hour's work.

–I'll have two Polish sausages.

–No you just get one because I already bought you a sloppy Joe.

– It's not where we are but where we were because that is where we are.

–Abba dabba dabba do.

–Phil, is Phil over there?

–Was there another guy sitting there?

–It's all an illusion.

–How could you miss ME? Not that I'm really

that vulnerable.  That noisy.

  –I'm in the middle of this desert with WHEELS. A sail with no wind.  Nowhere to go but sit here and SWAAK, and hope I'll be rescued.

  –John, you never seen a desert.

  –I AM THE DESERT WINDOW. On, on against the foe, draw the swords against the foe, swing along the desert wheel, sing on and on we go, you know, man.  Down with, uh, uh, whenever we're against, man, and up with us.  Leading forward, forward now we go into the desert reel.  Because I AM EL CORBALL, the great desert wheel! Just like Dennis Morgan and uh, uh, Lillian Thrush. Where were we? Out at the Key Club with Mickey Shaughnessy, would you say the contender for the late great Wallace Beery's place in moviedom? He was a hell of a cat, man, me and Charles one night…

  –The funniest thing he came out with tonight is that he was going to stage a Michael Rennie film festival.

  –Who's that?

  –Michael Rennie? Oh he's a neat old cat who played in uh, The Day The, uh, World Was Created, The Day The Earth Stood Still ... it was good. KLAATU BARADA NIKTO.  Michael Rennie's real claim to fame except for being Harry Lime on a TV. series now defunct about fifteen years that never made it in the first place, called The Third Man which was a marvelous movie, exemplary of Orson Welles, I didn't like it half as bad as my DOUG TAYLOR film festival.  That was my goal in life DOUG TAYLOR film festival.  Anybody here know who Doug Taylor is? Don't you remember the WILD BILL ELLIOTT movies of the forties?

Wild Bill always wore his guns backwards and was what they called a peaceable man. Doug Taylor, his side kick. 'Hey there, Wild Beel. I say HEY THERE, Wild Beel,' 'Hello there Cannonball, uh, what er yuh doin hyar in Laredo?' 'Wa-well. Wild Beel, I jes' coming on down hyar to uh, to see my Aunt Annie, the school marm.' 'Well there, uh Cannonball can yuh, uh, tell me a bout this hyar lawless element in this area of Texas? I've been sent here undercover, unbeknownst to anyone, I'm a U.S. Marshall.' 'Wow, Wild Beel I 'spect I can see what I can find.' 'Awright, Cannonball, but remember, I'm a peaceable man and I always wear my guns backwards, bone handles and all.' Much later in his career he became the late lamented Red Ryder of the serial fame.

–Who was little Beaver?

–Bobby Driscoll.

–Hand me that ash tray before I destroy the whole table.

John was wound up now, he was into his movies. Hey Jude plays in the background. Young Beatle-type college kids of Wichita are shooting pool. College militant blacks sitting around waiting to look angry. The kids were cool, going about their pool while the Old Guard sat yakking about old times. The 70's were coming up. Talking about the 50's, that was 20 years ago, John, Phil. John had spent twenty years watching television, rarely going out of the house. Maybe he sees an old cop who busted him for pills. "We never had those mind expanding drugs them kids are using now, John. They're dangerous. I know, you got on those pills, John, and I busted ya. They made ya a little crazy. But today, they're fooling with something dangerous." When we were goofin' there was just a handful of groovy people. Now it's groovy to be groovy. It's everyday. It's all changed. Twenty years, that's a long time to watch TV, John.

–Uh Bobby Driscoll is uh really known for about two roles. One was a Disney production, soul searching story of a southern colonial mansion fallen into disrepair.

–GHA! KHA! You heard about the midget Arab didn't you, Charley? You've heard about the midget Arab, Phil?

–No.

–Ah c'mon. Everybody knows about the midget Arab Why did the midget Arab never eat beans? Because every time he'd fart he'd blow sand in his shoes.

–Is that why they wear sandals?

–Where's Jimmy Mammy? Is he still in the joint?

–He had a straight forty-five years consecutive, man, and do you know how he got out? Good behavior playing baseball. Here's a habitual, out in two and a half years. He was their star outfielder and star runner, man. Jimmy Mammy the bear, man. Jimmy Mammy the bull.

–Then he got back in the joint?

–Well, let's see, he got out the summer before last, got him a new Mustang. He was driving those huge cement trucks, bigger than this room. Getting loaded on everything, every night. Come over to my house and stole two of my Wyamines one time, man. When I was ASLEEP. In fact he came in and told my mother, 'John wanted me to come in and wake him up.' He came in and woke me up, man, about three in the afternoon, man, he came in my door and said, John, you got anything?' I said, 'no, man, get out of here.' He said, C'mon let's go get some.' I said, 'no, man, I can't make it.' I went back to sleep. Okay man. I woke up, there he was ransacking my room with the door closed and my mother outside the house. I said, 'goddamit why don't you get out of here, you fucker.' He said, 'What!' 'What? I'm sorry man.' My mother was outside hanging out clothes, man. I went back to sleep, again, man. I thought he had left, man. I got up, stumbled out to the living room with my sleepy eyeballs and there's Jammy, alls he got on is his pants, shirts all over the room! Five or six of my shirts, hanging in between my eyes. He had tried them on, they were dirty, sweaty, I looked at him, I says, 'Goddamit Jammy!' I says, 'get out of here, man!' That son-of-a-bitch, I love him, man. My mother comes in. Says, 'what's going on here?' I said, 'get out of here, man.' He grabbed my shirt and started laughing, man, he fell out the door with my BEST SHIRT ON. My most expensive and newest and he jumped in his car, laughing as he drove off, left a dirty, filthy, rotten, smelly goddamn shirt he had on for nine days on top of a pile of other clean shirts he had crinkled up, man. And that's the last I'd seen him, I thought. I hadn't heard his NAME for about a month until one morning I happened to be a fine fellow that morning and off we went on a pot hunting expedition and I found some and I'm thinking, ah yes I'll give Jammy a little bit and get some goobers, I'll bargain with him for some goobers. So off we went in his Mustang, and while we're at this friend of mine's house Jammy walks in and lets me know out of the corner of his eyes that this friend has a very nice stereo and a very nice TV. set. He never locks his house. In the process of waving goodbye he had the set in the car. He went off to beat someone for some pills and said, 'I'll let you off right here, man, be right back, gonna score some pot.' He starts timing me. I ain't gonna go for it. I swear to god unbeknownst somehow or other, man, the door was open and I was standing there. I started timing him he was going three blocks and he'd be right back, under the pretext he was just going around the corner. I believed him. I swear to god, I believed him. In a half hour I glanced outside. I started fuming, I got so goddamn mad, man, I went home cursing him, thinking about it constantly. I would have conjured up a voodoo doll; I would have stuck things in it; I'd have set fire to it; I would have turned him in to the POLICE, man, I would have told them his name. I swear to god I'd have said he was in a red Mustang, he's got marijuana in the car and he's crazy drunk. But I just went home fuming all the more. The next morning on the Today Show on the local newscast picked up was James H. Jammy, convicted felon of numerous arrests, charged with drunken driving in a restricted area with no driver's license, marijuana in the car, open bottle, various and sundry kinds of pills, unidentified and is awaiting parole violation in the city jail here. I just went ha... ha, ha, ha. I started chuckling. First I thought, god no, then oh, wow, he'll never get out, then I chuckled a little louder, then I started hehawing. I laughed so hard. I was never so happy. I said out loud, I swear to god I sweared out loud, Jimmy Mammy you son-of-a-bitch, you deserve every year you get. I was a happy man that day, and I found out he only had to do a year in the county jail. This was about a year ago.

Johnny was wound up going on while the younger generation played pool. They were not interested in these stories. The juke box loudly: "All we are saying, is give peace a chance." Johnny talked loud above the juke box. The young people of the 70's looked very well kept beside John with his skin rash and hole in his cheek and almost blind eyes bulging toward irrelevant directions. Twenty years gone down the drain. Before long comes the little room and the pension check. Years pass like days. Sections of your life seem like chunks of fiction. Did I really do that or this? What was I thinking? Where was I? Where am I? Had better concentrate on getting my dirty socks down to the laundromat. Or a dozen eggs at the grocer's, there was nothing to recall then. All it was about was to live it. Then you talk to old people. They talk like they're behind an invisible wall. They talk as if they are taking their own picture apart from the immediate frame. Prophetic. Standing in the curtains. What they have can only be given and they are lucky to find a taker.

–What was that job you were working on with Jammy with those big drop hammers going: Whamp, uopt Whamp, uopt?

–Oh that was punch presses. Me and Jammy tried to steal some scrap metal there. We loaded it on the truck to go sell it and as we turned out

of the driveway it slid off all over the street. That
was like the time you and me was hustling the till
in men's wear dept. store Christmas rush. The
boss had his eye on you anyway, you weren't the
picture of propriety with your greasy duck's ass
haircut hanging over saturated collars. We stayed
high all the time and had benny sweat rolling
under our coats. He walked up and asked you
about a sale and you pulled out your charge book
with little rolled up dollar bills going everywhere
and you didn't even see them with your bad eye.

–Remember the time Big Indian got after
Jammy for stealing his chick's record player and
then selling it to him?

–AAAGHHH, yeah man, that was at long tall
Chris's pad, over on Shadybrook. There was a
bunch of us there that night. There was Jammy,
known as Bull Jammy, had the strength of fifteen
Gargantuas and the cods of a parakeet. We were
all there listening to records, five or six guys and
about that many chicks. A knock came to the
door. Who is it? Jimmy Jammy in there? Yeah,
just a minute. He went a step or two towards
the door but he didn't have to open it, because
there was a razor with a chain on the end of it
that had sliced the screen in one fell swoop,
wiped it from its roots, man, in the time of that
one action, every physical being in that room
had scurried all over that two room apt. They had
disintegrated, disappeared, and there he stood,
this HUGE INDIAN with a face of molten rock,
standing there with a chain in his hand, about
an eight foot chain with a straight razor on the
end of it. And that razor, when it touched any
object, part of the object went with it. It would

lash out like a viper's tongue, man, and whatever it touched it disintegrated it. It missed Jammy by about an inch and a half. All the objects in the room were being chopped in half. And all the occupants of the room went whoosh a room full of butterflies when the atom bomb goes off, man. In one fell swoop I was in the bathroom and another leap and I was behind the hot water heater. I stuffed myself in back of it looking out one good eye, and there was Spooly and you know how thin he is, and even HE was having trouble getting behind there. Three people dove under the bed at the same time, another hiding behind the drapes. One was behind the chest of drawers crouching down, another cat was in the kitchen with chairs pulled up against the kitchen table. In one swift motion Jammy was out the bedroom window, through the screen and onto the street. The Indian ran out to get him and Jammy shot past him like a cannonball. Jammy has legs about three feet shorter than mine, and I have no legs whatsoever, I have a stump on my body on each side with a foot hooked onto them. When I try to run or walk, I don't make too much progress. Jammy shot out of there like a goddam cannon with no shirt on, pants and shoes but no shirt, shot across the twenty foot yard in two steps, the third step in the middle of the street, the fourth step across the street and a couple of more he was a block and a half down the alley, with the Indian behind him with that chain a swinging, man, hitting the breeze and cutting twigs off trees and tops of picket fences. That all happened in about 20 to 30 seconds, the whole scene. Someone started coming out from behind chairs, from under the bed, from behind the divan.

Someone said what happened, who was that and what was that all about? And why? And wow, and then the discussion began, man and it got more volatile and more emotional and wow, that goddam Jammy did it again, man, whatever it was he did man, that's all there was to it. We forgot all about it, a couple hours later a cab pulls up out front somebody got out came up to the front door and said, 'hey, man, you got any money?' It was Jammy. 'You got any money, I have to pay this cab driver.' Still with no shirt on.

When champagne redeems the thought.  I know wherever I'm at if I go to a party in N.Y., Baltimore, San Francisco, Wichita or Tucumcari it will all be the same.  I will prepare myself for that new year's party of any year.  The party to begin a new decade where I stir and cry inside with that Isadora dance that never quits.  And there will be someone who remembers the twenties and they will bolt out of their chair and start dancing the Charleston like a demon of memory got hold of them for a flash.  Then someone will put Buddy Holly or Elvis or Joe Turner on and someone will be-bop out of a chair and up on the floor, remembering the days of yore and in a wild dance of the 50's Chuck Berry will sing the trance of memory through the wine.  The fire in the brain and the ache in the heart for more, MORE, MORE of anything whatever it was just so the reminder doesn't set in that it is a new year, a new decade. Then you realize that you're thirty, forty, fifty, sixty. Through each decade you stare. You feel like a sphinx peering through the same scene in a different era. Watching the girl with long blonde hair sit cross-legged in front of the scholar with a dark beard. She likes his eyes. He explains about relationships and experience. It will inevitably be open or aware or whatever the topic of the era. Oh my God does this follow one through one's natural life like a haunting joke at each party. The wispy one demands SOUL music so she can do her thing. She has done her black homework well. We will all get a chance to do our thing if there are enough parties left. The blonde says she likes my eyes. What shall I say. Oh God give me strength to rise up out of these bubbles and go home. To leave before the party is over because I couldn't take the ending of another party with the taste of eternity in my mouth and an unexplained gnawing hunger in my stomach.

Rapid Robert Ronnie Rasmutin Rannamuck, thief, artist, con man; alias Barbitol Bob, was standing in the dim lights of the Mona Lisa Club. He wore a silk shirt with a picture of a tree with its branches reaching over his shoulder and down his back. He wore a dark blue suit with baggy trousers. He was a bell hop subterranean hood with an Artaudian paranoia signaling from behind his flames and watch chains, a Lamantia-like silvery image of Christ and alchemical junkies of the asphalt corner of Crux and Fixes. (Crucifixes stuck into the long swan of eternity.) He was considering coming into a ring of petty criminals consisting of four pill heads, of which I was instigator and boss. We were layin some paper in the form of hot checks. Bob wanted to go to K.C. with us. He was drawing cartoons of gangsters and gun molls on the table. He was dreaming of building a house on some great lofty hill and living close to nature. He wanted also to go to art school. He sat there in the club with his hat pulled down to his eyes recording every action centimeter of the scene. The pockets of his one button roll were full of phone numbers and dope. His cufflinks glittered in the mirage madness of the colored lights, he was dreaming of that hillside where everything is flyspecked with glory, with the light through filtering the stained glass windows. The sun reflecting, illuminating his drawing paper with blotted gold, where thousands of faces formed without upkeep or care. No joy or history, nothing but infinite light. There he sat, St. Pimp, who saw a little too far behind the gaily painted door. I saw him later in the county jail. We traded some comic books and sent the screw for some Oxy. Outside the jail window a weary worker with his lunch pail waited for a bus under the streetlight in the center of America. Clinging on the trees over by the river bank the katydids chirped and sang in the spring air. The air was heavy with these locusts. Wichita was growing. Its cowtown beauty as lost as that ounce of gold dust swept from saloon floors down in the limestone beneath the asphalt forever. Wyatt Earp's grandson owns a used car lot. An oil portrait of Carry Nation hangs in the foyer of the ancient Hotel Eaton. In the latrine, old fairies purse their lips and crackle their dry limbs against their skins, Speed, space, and power, the forecast on the global wall. Bob went to the reform school. Summer rolled by. The next time I saw him I was sitting in Zip's Club. He saw

me and came over to my table. It was good to see
the thin faced painter con man again. We drank
beer and listened to the jive combo, scarfed a few
pills, and watched the gaiety of colors swirl in the
sparkling juke boxed pinball diamond dittybop
world of dingy dives. I had seen Jammy down
at the drug store on the corner Symphony Sid
used to call "the crossroad of America." Jammy
had just got out of the joint too. We were sitting
at the counter drinking coffee when Jammy
looked down at one of the fixtures which was
the base and stem of the barstool with no stool
upon it. He started laughing outloud to himself.
He pointed to the stem and said he knew some
guys in the joint who could sit down on it and
go all the way to the floor and never feel it.  Bob,
Jammy, and Big Indian left the club that night in
a T-Bird they had commandeered.  Big Indian
was feeling high and brave. He saw a Mack truck
coming down the highway. Only a crazy Indian
would have challenged it. His ancestral brain
was whirling against whatever force had trapped
him in an unfamiliar universe without salvation.
In one last brave yell the challenge of the vague
encroaching monster was seen in the truck. He
proclaimed he was not afraid of the big truck
coming toward him on the highway.  With Bob
and Jammy stone frozen in fear he pulled into
the oncoming lane and met the truck head on.
Jammy suffered a broken jaw, and Bob got all
his teeth knocked out. Big Indian lay dead with
his eyes staring at the heavens that refused him
shelter from the great white spider.

You either had to work all day for minimum
wage or you had to bum or steal.  If you stole the

odds were against you and you were too dumb
to realize it. If you were smart and stole you'd
probably become a well respected citizen. We
were none of these. Bob decided he should go to
college and naturally he didn't want to make the
scene by himself so he came over and got me one
day. I had been up for weeks and was in bed with
soup and crackers and lots of covers.

–Look here man, I can't go out there, I never
finished high school.

–Sure you can, you just got to fill out all them
papers and things.

Bob was very good in school and took his
art seriously. He took pride in belonging to
something official. They couldn't keep him out
of their ball game now, he was too good. I would
go to his house to see his latest paintings. Every
inch of his room was stacked with art. Pictures
from old magazines, cut-outs, globs of paint on
everything. He lived inside a Pollack painting.

Out at the Pioneer Club Big Nora jumped in
Bob's car and wheeled out of the parking lot and
ran over a rock. When he objected she reached
over and whopped him and told him to shut up.
That cigar smoking Wichita dyke wanted to fight
him anyway for dancing with her chick. Big Nora
even challenged Jammy to get out and fight her
one time when there was a dispute over who was
going to drive. Big Nora was the daughter of a
safecracker of the thirties. She thought of herself
as the original gun moll whip and stocking chick.
She was right out of Crumb's comics. Inside the
Pioneer Club Sonny was blowing his sax. Pack
Rat on the bass. His eyes closed in amphetamine
dream. His two front teeth curved down over his

lower lip. Tommy on the drums. Night Train and the stripper's big stocking legs urged forward like the rail that connects the two big locomotive wheels. A few pill heads zonked out, saying, "Go, man." And all night long Pillin' Pat the outlaw nodding her head. "Wail, man." After the joint closed we all went over to someone's house. Me, Jammy, John, Bob, Spoley Oley, Fast Car and Richard Rodent, the combo and the strippers. John was in the bathroom drinking coffee as the police came. Big Nora had Spoley squeezed in her arms. Everyone was goofin' smokin' poppin' pills. The police came, Big Nora ran out the door knocking cops out of her way and jumped in her brand new '53 Buick Skylark and peeled out of the driveway. "You ain't gonna get me, muthafucka," she yelled. Jammy crawled out of the window on to the roof. Fast Car pulled his gun and ran out in to the alley shooting into the sky. The police told the host it was a noisy party and he would have to put a stop to it. Sometime later one night Big Nora and I went down to colored town to get some barbeque. We were sitting in this joint when Big Nora looked through the window and saw the Black Maria pull up. She reached over and knocked me to the floor and fell on top of me under the booth. "Stay down honey, or they'll gun us down!" The cops came in after their coffee. I got up and wiped the barbeque sauce off and got out of her movie.

I made the scene out at the U. Bob was still illiterate but he took all art courses and consequently made all A's. He was in an art honors society. A fraternity asked him to pledge.

They called him and explained some of the
rules and started talking about housemothers.
"House what? You mean like man, there's some
dame around there gonna like, tell you when to
go to bed? Hey I don't think I'm going for this.
You'd better call Charley. Maybe he'd like to join."
I was not making good grades, though. In biology
for instance, I'd always get hung up. I liked the
sciences but they didn't like me. I tripped out
for days over the process by which a grain of
common table salt was formed. I usually had a
hangover or was comin' down off pills when I
went to the morning classes. I finally quit going to
a lot of classes and didn't bother dropping them.
I did very well in courses such as Metaphysics
or Business. Other than the Business College
(and I knew business, but couldn't transact it),
the other "catch all" fields were Sociology, Art,
Psychology, and English. Betty said Psychology
came into popular practice after World War II.
I checked out all these dull fields. At the bottom
of the pile was Education. I had always thought
of a Professor or a professional man as being
most distinguished, and I was shocked by their
generally low intelligence. I perceived that they
too could be little men, petty and unwise. They
could even slide into dim paranoia within their
department dynamics, their boundaries. What
was this new adventure I was to embark upon?
The trickster travels into another sphere. I
pretty well got a con going in the English racket.
It seemed somewhere I might survive in this
onslaught of reality that was going to face me
in the years to come. There were a lot of shits
in the department but I was to realize later this

had more or less to do with the total cosmic
or comic patchwork symmetry of life. Good
teachers are always under fire it seemed. Even if
it meant nothing more than tenure. Who knows
how many learned and professional idiots are
the product of teachers who were afraid of their
bosses. Afraid of not receiving tenure, afraid of
the ADMINISTRATION. I was going to see the
whole structure challenged in years to come, but
right now I had to content myself with my own
little rebellion at W.U. uttering dirty words and
terrorizing the English Department. I got to liking
art and poetry. There was an extremely creative
painter who presented, I should say, a Crusade
for Beauty. He was very knowledgeable of poetry
and music and had an immense appreciation
of them. He loved to teach these sorts of things
and always had some new poem or painting to
show me or some new piece to listen to. I got
turned on to Ezra Pound right away and started
writing poetry. I must admit there is something
about the image of the whole avant package
that can be kind of irksome but then one has to
start somewhere. I got an evening job running
an offset press. I told them I had experience. I
hadn't, but as I was to be alone with the machine,
the salesman showed me the basic switches, and
I learned to run it. I started training myself to
become an offset printer. I bought a house over
near the school where I lived with Rocks, Bruce,
and Crandal. We all had an intense dedication to
the arts.

Betty came back for a visit, got a job in an
office. I showed her around spade town. She got
to know a club owner where we always went.

She poured her drink over some guy's head and called him nigger muthafucker. She had a bad habit of doing that which always made those around her a little uneasy. She terrorized the town and then split for Green River, Wyoming, one of her favorite towns. She got that feeling to go and stepped right out on N. Broadway, hailed a truck and was gone.

I lay over in my house on Stadium Drive and listened to music. I drank a lot of cough syrup, smoked pot when it was available, took peyote. I had a box full of peyote, it had started growing out of itself, the old flesh of the plant was becoming withered and drawn. On the top of the plant was a kind of cotton-like fuzz sticking up like time frozen ejaculation rays— and out of them came new limbs, new buds, new lives. Ronnie had brought over this old spade musician who wanted to see some of that PI-I-o-TEE. "Hey, man looky here, I mean," he says, "you got something that make you have them visions. You see things in your mind. I want to dig some of that shit, man." I went and got two or three of the scaly green buttons with the mangy hag root twisting down like a tornado. The fir and the new buds. I started to hand them to him. He pulled his hand back, jumped back and said, "HUNH-UN man, no sir," and he took a handkerchief out of his pocket and wrapped it around his hand before he took one. The plant was as green and wrinkled as the music present in his brow. There seemed to be a miniature peyote cult among those who frequented my house. I think one of the first times I saw Alan (not to be mistaken for Allen who appears later on) that is A-L-A-N, as Neal would make a point of announcing after Alan had spelled it for him upon meeting; I saw him light on my screen door one day. He swooped onto the door like a crazed rabbit and clung there an instant kind of spread-eagled like. He had come from a friend's house, home from Mexico; and he was all Blissful and Illuminating in Spring-Hart Crane-like fits. He carried some poems on paper or in his mind like one his friend had written—the image of a wife stained kitchen view. And now comes summer which will be hot, hot. I took a swig of Gallo Port. Instant Rot. Alan and I were always going to do THE LITTLE MAGAZINE to which I was always going to appoint him editor, and which I never did. I always printed long poems of my own instead. We drank peyote green bile straight from the devil's asshole, and smoked weed and speculated through the interior cosmic monologue. We drank the wine of youth. We went to parties where we pissed between a girl's legs who was sitting on the john. We took off our clothes and rolled around naked with this chick, Alan with supreme delight asked her to take off her belt and whip him. She fucked him and wanted me to fuck her under the arm. I came all over both of them. We went to another party where dykes and fags had painted each other green and purple and had started fist fighting. Alan was from a different background than me. He resembled Billy the Kid whose mother was actually on the committee that chartered early Wichita. Alan came out from N.Y. just like Billy. Alan always told me his name was "Billy Jiddy" which was a corruption of "Village Idiot."

Sometimes he signed his writing "Billy Jiddy."
Anyway Alan was a child poet genius who bore a
resemblance to Billy the Kid, Rimbaud, and Hart
Crane all put together. He had difficulty at times
fitting all the little bits of universe together which
would prompt Rocks to yell: "Jesus Christ, Alan,
do I have to explain the whole world to you?"
We listened to Flamenco, Raga, Verdi, Puccini,
Caruso, Bartok, Bach, Mozart all the time hour
after hour and read poetry. Someone brought a
book of this cat who was out in San Francisco.
He was honest, he was saying something. Out of
the old bohemia with beard and heavy silver ring
into the sidewalk cafes of North Beach. Bob had
gone out to Frisco earlier. I stayed around and
went to Wichita U. some more. I wanted to be a
Jet Pilot and went to the R.O.T.C. I did well as a
drill sergeant and we soon formed a crack drill
team. That is the age where you crack the mold
or end up some kind of flaccid mommy's boy-
the warrior type-officer. I declared war obsolete
and insane; its very nature the absolute evil of
apocalyptic runaway paradox. The dye is cast,
babes. We passed review with drums blaring,
rifle butts jutting, shiny black shoes flashing just
like my emotion, like I was on Speed or Bennies,
a great elation, the sick sadistic Hitler buzz like
children get when they squeeze cats or whip
chickens, that ritualistic climax of power that
prods us onward, lost in syndromes, the great
nordic energy eager to lie in a heap of untanned
skins, as if dying is not enough. I found a piece
by Einstein which went something like anyone
who marches rank and file to a bombast of
patriotism has been given his great brain by

mistake, his spinal chord would have sufficed. Now I knew I could tell them at the draft board they were insane. Of course this automatically made me insane. I went to the shrink to get a 4-F. I told him some of the deeper points in the whole cosmic set-up. Mankind wants to kill. His reason is deeper than the grey mist of chromosome. He will continue killing until he has courage to face a miracle. The wars won't end with treaties and pacts. There will be no surrenders no victories nor losses. The war will end when a miracle happens to mankind. Patriotism and peace talks with animal sounds of troops who are equipping themselves for war but form an eight-rayed star rotating to the left. The karma at ghost dance has served. The star is not in the sky and not a diamond, but a configuration on the earth formed by human beings. He was willing to write me a letter to Larned, Menninger, anywhere but his clinic. He had his own cluster going. I went down to the draft board with this pot smoking sheriff minister of this small town who was also a folk singer. We went over to Bob's house in his sheriff's car with red lights, the whole thing. Bob wouldn't come to the door. I went to get him saying it's cool man, c'mon out. He finally got near enough to the car, and I took out a joint, lit it right in front of this sheriff and offered Bob a toke. Bob split into the house all freaked out, in a total fit of paranoia. That was a dirty trick all right, on our way to the draft board, arriving there to make the clerk have a nervous breakdown I threw open the doors and asked them if they were hiring any killers. I told them I KNEW they were meeting in that other room, saying that

I couldn't get into the army. I am physically
fit, why can't I go. They're trying to say there's
something wrong with me. The pot smoking
folk singing preacher sheriff was explaining and
making up a case as he went along. I yelled with
Lee Marvin bravado, are you hiring any killers?
After World War II the army began to be more of a
personality mutation, don't you think? Gimme a
gun, I want to kill for peace! I want to fire mortar
on the mess hall! I want to eat a General Hershey
Bar! I know you're conspiring to keep me out of
the army. They gave me a permanent 4-F. But it
really didn't make much difference. Later in life
I may wish I had more experiences to exhaust.
Everything got all experienced up so fast I ran
out of things to pad experience with. I started
to taste re-occurrence of a reality dream. The
proper lessons and byways and disputes forever.
Familiar archetypes cruise past the doorways of
the minds. Street boys swim hawking papers.
The eel with a boy's head down the flowing
street. Look at those Giotto eyes that stare from
the canvas. Pictures of Hitler Youth. Sickness
cultivated like the goose liver. That's how they
make goose liver or liverwurst. They nail the
goose's feet to a board so they don't move then
they force feed the dough and tie rubber bands
around their necks so they can't spit it back up.
They can't get any exercise and are stuffed so the
liver gets abnormal and soft and festered up. The
youth eyes of weird male worship cult. Like the
early swastika made up of these four figures on
hands and knees with nose to ass. This squint
eyed ignorance, you see it in the cities, in the
suburbs. Hart Crane described the idiot "with

the squint lanterns in his head."

Occasionally I would take time out from higher education and go to tent meetings or revival meetings with my sisters. A huge tent out on a vacant lot. The cars started arriving, a Ford with rods knocking, a Chevrolet with a banged up fender, cars and caravans of those to be healed. They came from farms where butter is churned and reality is a new implement. They came from cheap apartments on N. Main or N. Water. They drove from their homes to see the man with the miracle arm. There in a regal suit sleeve was a stiff arm that miraculously welded itself back together when it got shot off in the war or something. The whole angel of mercy scene with the cross and shield and sword. They came from all around. Okies, Arkies, Jayhawkers, winos, dementias, old women swelling with emotion, jumping in the air falling on children, shaking, waving, speaking in tongues, united crucial grey mists of ritual. They came in the mud, in the wind of refuse, swooned, devoured, impoverished, depleted and drained they walked on rainbow bridges while the organ wailed in praise; they walked among the casts, sat among the wheelchairs, knelt along the stretchers. He held out his miracle arm to touch the infirm, he exonerated the innocent predator. He forgave the hyena and the werewolf. The snarling blast of promise blowing in the vast corners of the tent. The guardian Angel, the convict, the backslider the locust, the maddog and the rogue elephant lifted up to joy without terror. The beast was freed. The limbs of nearby trees crackled and snapped under the weight of harpies and furies, vampires and wasps. Here were the poor, the downtrodden yearning to be free redeemed from this world of chimeric miseries. A savage vulture points to a spot on the ground illuminated in red. An outlaw bitch flourished in a trance of swirling balls of worship. A dreamer would like to run away but he could not do so. He is trapped by the magnet of psychic blood. His palms begin to sweat. He feels someone behind him looking at his flush neck. One of the children turns into an animal and bites him on the calf. The mother falls to the ground in a state of ecstasy. Someone takes an envelope of money up to the man with the miracle arm. He moans and shouts at the crowd to raise their arms. Some jump up and cry and scream in tongues. The infirm and lame press toward him to be touched. Altlyamammn Lanyannt yannt rurteyaa gianta laminnya sabba. Raise your arms to the lord. The fingertips were stretched toward heaven. Mass thwarted energy burst through the fingernails to touch God. To be reborn. The touch through the circus tent under the Kansas stars. Raw energy flowing. RAISE YOUR ARMS! RAISE YOUR ARMS! The magnetic pitch was rising. Everyone began raising their arms, fluttering their hands in the sky. All at once a big rat ran under the bench where one of my sisters was sitting. She saw the rat and screamed to us to RAISE YOUR LEGS! RAISE YOUR LEGS! My other sister thought she had got hold of the spirit itself!

And back to my house near the University I lay with my head against the Hi-Fi. I drank a lot of cough syrup which was the old standby junky kick.  It wasn't too much compared to the drugs nowadays but I managed to sink into some syrupy raga on the Hi-Fi.  Sometimes this black lady would strut down the street. I invited her in. She wanted some beer and I told her to sit tight. I ran next door to a friend's house who was talking with his girl about plays. I went in the door and opened his refrigerator took some beer and left. He didn't even see me. Bob and I paid this lady to fuck us. We asked her if she would like to get fucked in the ass and the cunt at the same time. She said yes and apparently didn't care.  Bob started fucking her in her ass while I tried to get my prick in her.  She started laughing with me at the situation, but we managed to get something going. We all got drunk and then went to sleep. Next door a Hi-Fi blared into the dawn. Rocks had his machine on full force playing Beethoven and Mabel Mercer.  He had been out with a sixty year-old woman he was going in the oil business with. He had an oil worker's hard hat in the back of his car and his shoe split down the back. I had met Rocks a few weeks before in a tavern. I told him I was studying Philosophy.  He said he knew something about entelechy and handed me this paper he had written on it.

MW Galactic Region
104 Solar, Planet 3
Second Quarto Hemisphere
Elevation 12, 5th Sector
Ist T. O., 0900

SUBJECT: Entelechy
TO: Induced Realization System Affected

RE: lst Appraisal

This is to inform you that the consequences of your every pulse are now monitored thru diurnal parallax and supportive configurations at the Quarto-hemispherical Tabulation Relay Point-known as QTRP. The engram of this interplasmic combo-circuit differentiates itself quite easily from the Simulated Human Response Systems commonly in use at this time-known as SHRS'S. The possible resultant is a complete breakdown in the QTRPs ability to run monitor data on an individual basis. The switchover will then become automatic to Entity Melding Whole Visualization Procedure-EMWVP. We hope of course that the implementation of EMWVP will seldom eventuate.

Sustained reliance upon EMWVP necessitates the call-up thru the Primeval Symbols and Archetypal Image Archive of obsolete form-patterns to be sent up to Gross Terrestrial Relay Point for referral to Conditioned Solar Replicating Center for Annotated Cellular Synthesis and Catalogued Circuit Formulation. And this can only be expected to effect a temporary sub-identification holding pattern sufficient to allow you to continue functioning in your present form, without cross psycholizing and partial Identity-Loss.

As you know Identity-Loss remains the greatest threat to consciousable existence. I am sure that you do not wish to be switched from self-motivated consciousable response to Servo-Programmed Circuit Response. It has been conclusively established that entities in your present form are more adaptable to

Interstellar Motilities than Identifications of any other previous order. It is to be hoped that by apprising you of the fact that your active space-time physicality and psychocircuital procedure are being monitored by QTRP and that you may run the risk of being sensitized by the Systems mentioned in order to preclude Identity-Loss in your present form, will sufficiently induce you to begin reprogramming your present psychocircuital directions.

Thank you for your attention.

ISCCD Gamma Psi - A

He was in a Geology class I was in and we sat next to each other. He rarely came to class and when he did he delivered a lecture on weather, wind velocity, earth formation, whatever. I think we both flunked the course.  He was sitting at a table in the tavern when I walked by.  He was very hostile and asked if I thought he was homosexual. Then he talked about bronc busting and I told him I had ridden in rodeos too. He talked about living in Ulysses, Kansas and I told him I had lived there. He talked about working on oil wells and I told him that I had too. Then he got very mad and wanted to fight. He thought I was putting him on.  Then he kept thinking that I thought he was queer.  Then he flipped back into a story of driving his car as fast as it would go out over the deep Colorado plateau where there was nothing in the immensity of the dark night except the speeding thrill of insect odometers registering the impulses of black reality under the moon. Rocks got onto a subject and he would research it all the way.  We both enrolled in an

English course and the first thing he did was to go to the library and check out dozens of books on space. He knew all the specifications of missiles. He got into it so much he never came to the English course except to recite SAILING TO BYZANTIUM. He took off for Denver and returned in time for the final. I went by his house to remind him and he woke up, got dressed, and went over to school. He was reported to have had 149 hours of Fs. and he had to be re-instated in school several times. Most of his subjects related to the 17th century or to the time he spent racing Austin-Healeys in Germany. He had just come in from somewhere and was all keyed up. He knocked a hole through the wall and then left to get some beer. You could always hear him peel rubber as he drove out of the driveway. He returned quickly and sat down at the typewriter. About as long as it took to put the paper in and take it out, he composed the following poem, reading it over and over with glee,

"Across the street
And under the tree
My dog sits upon a spider I caught.
Tomorrow I must take my spider to bath
And wash it clean.
My dog doesn't know my spider is dirty"

Rocks jumped into his car and sped out onto the ice and snow. We had picked up Bob and we sped home from spadetown. Rocks went 50 and 60 on the icy city streets. He barely clipped rows of cars just driving so he would barely touch them. Bob said, "hey, man, like let me out this next corner. I don't care how cold it is, I'm going to walk home." Rocks hit the second gear so hard he broke the gear shift off his car. The clutch pedal was rammed through the floor. He went home one night and chopped the toilet seat in half. He took a meat axe to it. He took a gun and pulled the fat around his middle between his fingers and wanted to shoot it off. "The flaunting, fleshy mechanism." He jumped in his car and sped into the night. Rocks became somewhat of an expert in any field that happened to occupy his mind. If he found a particular passage of Mozart he admired he would listen to ALL of Mozart. He would not rest until he acquired everything available that was written about Mozart. Then he would talk to music majors, much to their amazement about particulars in the music. He wrote a lot and about a great variety of things. He treated his writing and the fat around his stomach with the same resentment. As a world traveler, he was of course a master wine taster, that was not the opinion, however, of Lawrence Ferlinghetti. Larry had asked to see some of Rocks' poetry and I finally got them together for a meeting. The subject got onto wine, and apparently lasted all day with them drinking and arguing about wines. When I saw Rocks again I heard his version of how he tried to illuminate Larry on the subject of wine. When I saw Larry again he said he knew something about wines himself, and that he didn't share Rocks' views on wines. That kind of ended the prospect of having Rocks' poems published but he didn't care. A year or so before, I had read Rocks' poetry to a group at the Gough St. flat. Dave Haselwood, who owned Auerhahn Press at the time was delighted with Rocks' work and suggested we go down to his press and set

and run a small edition of his poetry, which we
did. But Rocks did not go to San Francisco on
account of poetry. When he did come there he
dropped in regularly wherever I lived. I guess
he left Wichita for many reasons, but he ended
up reuniting with all his friends who had fled
Wichita for San Francisco. In the Wichita days
though, Rocks was staying at my house. We had
begun to have kind of marathon parties because
there wasn't too much else to do there. My place
soon became a place of curiosity for the unwary
sorority girls and eager art students. Rocks had
a record collection of from three to five hundred
albums and about that many books. He spoke
with compulsion and read in convulsions. The
parties began to grow out of the door and onto
the street. The mad anxiety of someplace to go
had leaked out into the academic community.
Sometimes there were cars jammed all along the
block and had to spill over into the University
parking lot. Then over the years after the first
wave of wild men left Wichita, the parties still
grew and grew. Kegs of beer, bottles of wine,
acres of weed, handfuls of speed. The carnival
bulged and expanded stretching the limits of
reality until everyone was lost unto themselves
again forever, knowing that they must leave from
the same universal door they came in. Tomorrow
will be the ordinary day with orderly time and
space. No! This party will go on through eternity.
The Red Faced Puker will come. He will show
up and puke all over the place. The ceremony
of indulgence will begin. The nausea will press
inside the flesh. The balloon man will swell with
anxiety nausea. The vortex will take root in the

brain and swim alone out into the black sky. The sickness of excess will bulge in the liver. The drunkenness will feel like an enema stuck up the ass with the water flowing in. Time will swell. The Red Faced Puker is upon us. It is time to sober up, it is time to see Grandmother's Reality Meadow, the Sunday afternoon time element in a Seurat painting, the safe impression science can verify.

Art reached the vast cultural desert of Wichita, though not much of the real stuff trickled in, and when it did we clung to it religiously. A Beckett recording on the record player would be listened to over and over. If we wanted more, we had to create our own. We had to have fluid all the time on the desert. Art was a privilege. Something to bring the strugglers together. We were like innocents or primitives looking with awe upon the great god Art. We never quit a day without finding and experiencing a new poem or piece of music or a painting. There was not much art upon the plains. You had to see the wash of a sunset for a painting and look at it in a museum without walls.

On especially sunny days, I would see a little blonde lightly walking skipping toward my house, her ponytail bouncing back and forth. She had the rare beauty of a fawn with big brown eyes. She seemed to me the living song of Keats' La Belle Dame Sans Merci. I had written her a poem because of her outstanding beauty and then tried to stay anonymous, but at the same time letting her know where I could be sought out. I had just begun writing poetry and had already used it to get a piece of ass. The shame of a poet and the pact with the Muse. She had to trap anyone she could to help absorb the weight of beauty, a terrible thing in itself to know, and then to pretend yourself into existence! Her friend, a very beautiful dark Spanish-looking girl, came with her sometimes and we would perform the Rites of Spring. We would put a record of Vivaldi on, and I would play the Satyr for them by prancing around naked with a hard-on. They would undress each other, one exposing the other's beautiful pink nipples with the honey hair falling softly upon them. And the other's breasts fuller yet and brown, the kind you could suck hard with your mouth and pull with your fingers until the earth woman sighed with pain. Then the air woman would kiss them in camaraderie, as she ran her cool fingers of lake water down into the other's fiery deep rose. I slipped her panties off her ass and kissed her thighs as she removed the earth woman's. I saw her fine pubic hair glisten in the sunlight, and fantasied with her underwear delicately placing it on my cock and over my face inhaling the perfumed fragrance of it, pretending that is all I had of them, prolonging the great prize I knew was mine. I masturbated as they lay upon the pad on the floor and fondled each other for my benefit. I changed the record and put on some raga as the air girl ran her slim white fingers against the clitoris of the earth woman. She spread her own legs apart and I pulled the sides wide apart stretching the skin taut over the clitoris. I touched my tongue to it and then buried my face in the warm pink. Then I slipped my tongue down firmly into her asshole and she writhed with pleasure and spread her cunt as wide as possible with her fingers while earth woman pressed her hot tongue into it like a bumble bee upon a rose. I slid my cock into earth woman's hot womb and kept my face buried in air girl. Then we changed around until we were all covered with wet sex and exhausted and richly satisfied.

Summer came and Bob wanted to go to harvest. He talked me into it saying how good it would be to be out in the open. We went out to western Kansas. The wheat wasn't ripe yet so we headed down to the panhandle of Oklahoma. We hit the local cafes and beer joints to get word of crews being formed. We heard that a guy out in a cabin camp at the edge of town needed some extra hands. We went to hire on and he had heard of my father so he put me to work driving a combine. Bob went on another crew that was helping him. He was to drive a truck. Bob hadn't done anything like that before, being a city boy, but he wanted more than anything to become the type of rugged individual that mastered the elements and made things grow and didn't have to depend upon anyone else. In Kansas my father showed him the house he had just finished. He found a spot and bought the land. He got on his bulldozer and scooped out a foundation. Then he got in his truck and hauled bricks from Wichita and supervised the bricklayers. He designed his own house to suit him. Then he did the landscaping and planted trees. Inside each brick pillar around the porch he had put a steel pipe and ran it full of concrete. He made things to last. Bob liked the idea of the farmer who had to be an expert banker and economist to keep up with the market. He also had to be a top mechanic when a combine or tractor broke down. It amazed Bob to see someone do a major repair job on a combine right there in the fields. Every part was taken out and cleaned until the broken part was discovered. Then someone would go to town and get the new part and come back and put the whole thing back together. The farmer also had to be an expert in animal husbandry, a vet, a carpenter, a grower. This fascinated Bob, all these projects and problems to be solved and no one telling you how. You just found a way and did it, and that was that. He also enjoyed the personalities and character of these rough and rugged people. He watched everything with his artistic eye. It was something he never had in the city streets or in the joint. But as fate would have it, just like the face of reality had been shit in, Bob started working for this kind and gentle old man and his faithful one-armed hired hand. And if anyone needed a good hand it was he. His machinery was kind of old but good, but in a tough, fast situation such as custom cutting you couldn't take any chances. It was too easy to lose your shirt. They didn't have those new red hot hungry self-propelled jobs that would eat up a field of wheat in a day, pouring it into new, fast, rugged trucks that drove right alongside while the wheat poured, never losing time. They had old machines that needed the most experienced to make them pay. And they got Bob. It so happened that the fellow Bob was working for contracted a little work from the fellow I worked for. The boss started yelling at about 4:30 that morning. We had just gotten to sleep. We staggered bleary-eyed out of bed thinking to hell with it, we'd rather bum. We got into our clothes as the boss yelled for us to hurry. Then we went to a cafe to eat breakfast, filled the water cans and went to the field. We pulled in behind my boss who was in his truck with a giant combine on the back of it. It stood high in the air, hung over both sides of the truck and drooped off the back. The big international harvester which could cut a swath and chew the wheat head and spit out the seeds faster than millions of peasants threshing wheat the rest of their lives. You would see a whole line of these giant metallic grasshoppers on the trucks along the highways. Bob and I were in the car and pulled in behind the boss and his rig so we could follow him out to the field. We heard the shriek of air horns and I looked in the mirror to see one of these giant rigs descending upon us. I caught a glimpse of fat cigar and fist shaking at us as the rig swerved into the passing lane and highballed it around us, open throttle. I slowed and pulled meekly to the shoulder as he cut in front of us. We drove down the road in the cool of the morning. The sun was out and then we felt a light gust of warm air swimming past us.

–Gonna be a scorcher today.

–Yea.

–Gonna be a scorcher.

The golden ripe wheat wavered in the sun. Clashed like metal someone said? The smell of the golden blue red morning. The churning of the hill over silver bleak stone. Sunrise washes clear a fresh face, beneath the dried tears of last night's sorrow when the angel of death cupped its hands to the miracle of life and drank. o religious

morning brilliant through the treetops, frozen
silver honey, the feel of a new day! Wagon train
in shiny metal crossing the plains. Trail master
high in his cab of truck out in front. Shaking,
grinding, roaring, rolling big truck tires singing.
It was about noon before we reached the field
we were going to cut. The trucks backed down
in the barpit, the combines driven right off the
trucks. The ground was hot and dusty through
your boots. You would leave a trail of silt and
dust. Terrible metallic insects built to survive
the brutal plains swooped down upon you and
bit out tiny chunks of flesh. Noon glittered like
knifeblade. The heat left ripples in the mirage of
dizziness. Sweat drenched the face. We found
a place in the shade of an old building where
we could hunker down or stand for a while and
bullshit. Abruptly in the dust a shiny red truck
appeared, its front wheels cocked and skidded
to a stop. The driver climbed down from the cab
and strolled up to us gouging crusts of dirt and
grease from under his fingernails with his huge
worn penknife.

–You got in my place.

–What?

–You got in my place. Behind the boss. On the
highway.

–Oh. I didn't know it was yours.

He was tall and had a pockmarked face. He
wore black boots with an eagle inlay and fancy
stitching. He had his good pair in the cab. He
wore dirty black western cut pants with a pearl
button on the flap. The lines of his face were
etched by double chromosomes. His black pants
were stuffed into his boots. He was wearing a

black cowboy shirt with pearl buttons. In his pockets were Roi-Tan cigars, ballpoint pens, and gauges. He had a black handkerchief around his neck. He looked like Jack Paladin. On his black belt was a decorative silver buckle representing the icon of a truck. His hat was also black with a silvery stretch band around it. There were pins on his hat suggesting and confirming various different chauffeur and truck driver locals all the way from Florida to Alaska. As he stuck his black gloves in his back pocket, Bob turned to me and said, "He's a Double Duty Dandy." Bob made fast friends with Double Duty because he knew this guru of the grasshoppers was someone who knew the ropes when it came to driving trucks. Lunch time came and we were starved. We hadn't seen food since daybreak. Bob was thinking about all that fried chicken, mashed potatoes, gravy, string beans topped off with some apple pie and iced tea. He went over to his boss and they opened a can of Vienna sausages and ate them with white bread. There was another selection: baloney and bread, or what they called "dog."

–Milk or coffee?

–Milk.

The blow dust swirled up under our footprints. The hot straw flew as the combines chopped away. I crawled into the cockpit of one of the combines, put on a pair of goggles and pulled the brim of my straw hat down. I lowered the reaper and it ate a huge swath into the field of wheat. Its parts chugged and shook and ground and wobbled and rolled. I saw Bob load up his old Ford truck for this poor old guy. He headed for the barpit to cross in order to get on the highway.

He had a full load of wheat. As an old hand would know, you would have to drive into and out of the ditch at an angle in order to get more traction out of your pulling wheels and avoid being "high centered" where the wheels would be down in the bottom and the bed and frame would be into the ground. Also a lot of wheat would spill. It was against the code of manhood to give a greenhorn any valuable advice, at least until he had made a mistake or two. I guess this was because any liaison had to fall first in a need, a sympathetic need and the greenhorn would have to grow into the code; otherwise the code itself may make a mistake and select unto itself someone not worthy. A cad, a showoff, a ding-a-ling, a squirrel, an asshole. Double Duty squinted in the sun as he kept a keen condescending eye on Bob's truck. His face was smug as his badges danced in the sun. The Black Knight of the grasshoppers in his red machine. Bob's truck went head on into the ditch and got stuck. Sweat began to rise around Double Duty's black sideburns. He curled his mustache and with disdain watched the wheat pour from Bob's truck. He was happy though at the chance to be a hero. He jumped in his truck and shoved it in gear and spun to the rescue. The next thing that happened to Bob's truck is that the brakes went out. And then a flat tire. After that Bob got lost and Double Duty set out to find him, and never missed his turn at loading. All this time the Kind Old Man and the Faithful One Armed Hired Hand were occupied with keeping the combine functioning.

One time we weren't busy for a spell and Double Duty shared with us some of his secret loves. He pointed to the spotlights he had just bought for the truck. They flashed in the chromium sun. He had just bought them payday. He told us of the air-horns he had bought last payday. He spent most of his money on his boss' truck. His boss wisely let him feel the truck was his and he could do what he wished with it. The boss gladly drove the old one. Double Duty would tell us stories of driving. He would pat his truck and tell us how much weight she'd carry and how fast she'd go. And he let us know that he had the privilege of driving it as hard and fast as he wanted. On Sundays he would wash it. The boss didn't have to pay for his board because at night he would sleep on his truck. He slept wherever his truck slept, and covered himself with his tarp. What were his dreams out under the huge starry Kansas sky? What bar girl did he leave behind? What life had he fashioned for himself in these great United States? He rested. The guru of the grasshoppers. They will hum to him the dry membrane oracle. A vague spinning wheel sounds in the ghost air. At intervals there is the accompaniment of shrill metallic clicking. "The wind moves above the wheat/With a silver crashing,/A thin war of metal." The poet said.

The next day Bob lost his way to the elevator and Double Duty went after him. If Fate ever dealt a bad hand it did that time to the Poor Old Custom Cutter and his Faithful One-Armed Hired Man. It was getting dark and it looked like a storm was brewin', I had been on the combine all day in the hot sun, sweat and wheat chafe pouring down my neck and mixing with hot dust that filtered through my clothing and settled in

my folds. I had a sunburnt nose and bites from
huge undefinable flying insects. We got in the
boss' pickup and drove into town. It was dark and
he stopped by the grain elevator to drink some
beer and shoot the shit. It seemed late to me by
the time we got home. I regained a kind of third
consciousness through fatigue and misery, and I
got to where I didn't care what was happening. I
felt like I had been up for days on bennies. I could
have fought, fucked, robbed a bank, shot up the
town, anything—after battling the elements all
day—it would be just another state of suspended
electrically charged animation. We got back to
the cabins and we needed some beer, but we
were busted. I told Bob to hit on Faithful Hired
Hand for some bread until payday. After much
hesitation and deliberation Faithful dug deep
in his pocket and slipped a five dollar bill out
of hidden compartments of his billfold. He told
us to be sure and not tell the boss he had it. He
didn't want the boss to know he had any money.
This was his savings. The ratholed fin. I sent Bob
after some beer and we drunk ourselves into a
stupor. We were ready for oblivious rest. The
windows of the cabin were broken out and the
smell of rain and storm on the prairie saturated
our senses with beautiful energy fragrances.
This was one of the extreme compensations that
repay oneself for one's discomfort. It was always
like that on the plains. We finally went to bed
for a short fitful rest until all of a sudden some
kind of animal, a skunk or huge rat or beaver
jumped in bed with us and got entangled within
the covers. Flaying arms and legs, Bob jumped
up to turn on the lights as we caught a glimpse

of it jumping out the window. We got settled down after that, but outside burned an accursed fiery light bulb. Not only that, but the dry noise and shadows of thousands of winged creatures buzzing around the world of light. Bats with shrunken dogs' heads hanging upside-down in acrobatic silence of the phantom beams peering into the mad whirl of the metropolis born in darkness and circling the Great Artificial Light. Great green grasshoppers pivot their necks toward the Metropol of light. Outside the realities of sound, outside the senses came that first condition of beauty. That sense of order of the flower pots along one hundred window sills. The incestuous rejoicing of the cockroach and the fly. The long search of the centipede around the dingy faucet sewers. The female Mantis in her cannibal feasts of lovers. The hop toad's tongue and the hoot owl's round gold eyes take in this blur of life around the globe-ancient lantern swinging round out of control. Treasures from the past and future. I drank some more beer. I could not sleep. I put the light out and tried to go back to sleep. The cabin camp manager came back and turned it on. I got up, dressed, and told Bob he's got to go get the manager for me. I spoke in low deadly tones. I didn't trust myself alone with the manager. He was scrawny and stupid, just right for me to take out all my accumulated aggressions on. I spoke in a low deadly voice and asked Bob to summon the manager. He came up to the door of our cabin where the light burned. I explained very precisely that we could not sleep because of the light. He said he had to have it on. I started thinking of reasons he would have to have it on just to try to entertain myself so I would not rip into him and hit him with all the fury I had absorbed that day. He said he had to have the light on to keep the Indians away.

–They come up and carry the place away!

–What?

–They'll come and carry it away!

–They'll attack? Well how the hell is that fucking light bulb gonna keep them away? All they gotta do is come through those goddamn windows that are completely broken, and all the fucking animals come in, for Christ-sake, you fucking son-of-a-bitch. What you mean the Indians will get you?

Bob was trying to calm me down, thinking the guy might be able to do us trouble. I'm alternating between fits of laughter and violent threats to this squirrelly motherfucker.

Bob and I followed the harvest on to Kansas where he stuck it out and was hired by a farmer to drive a tractor. I went on back to Wichita.

Bruce, a painter, had a problem with space. Time too, I suppose. Although Neal said I had a problem with time. Bruce would always think it peculiar that we could be at one place and then know we were going to be in another place after a while. Like we would plan to go over to the concert. He could imagine us there— thinking about where we were before. I started to see the way an artist looked at things. Before there was just one dimension, and now there are two. One/Two. That long lost eve we sat at the concert. Everything was uncomfortable, tight. The performing artists of Wichita U. were

about to play. Someone goofed drastically and
the wrong notes threw an electric curtain over
the audience. Bruce was always sensitive to
embarrassing situations so he thought he was
personally responsible. He envisioned people
peering at the back of his neck. We wanted to
roll in laughter but repressed it to the point
of pain. Now his face grew red. I had a sickly
expression like a dog looks when it takes a shit.
Oh I wanted to laugh, and had to keep moving
my jaws, rubbing my eyes, anything to help hide
the fact that I was about to crack open with mad
laughter. We sweated through the performance.
I thought a lot about art those days, I developed
the realization that an artist, painter, or writer
had a dual purpose. He was, and he watched
himself become–he is, and watching himself
be. He can never go back to just being, doing
the things before him, an organized task to
perform. A logical stay through eternity. Oh my
god! Now I have to see myself and this whole
thing differently! I have to watch what I do.
Then of course the paranoia! But never again
free to perform tasks without thinking about it
altogether as an artist would. The actors, I know
they forget who they are. And the painters, they
perceive in a dual reality, the form put together
from many pieces, and then the writer or poet
always stands apart from it, observing it. I didn't
want to sit there, or anywhere writhing in mad
laughter, grunting in my own obscurity. And
then I started thinking about life, or death, or
whatever you call it. Sometimes thinking now
I'm here. Someday I won't be here. Where will I
be? It's just like living in a hotel room.

Bruce and I took off for Guadalajara, Old Mexico in his '52 Ford. Out in the pitch black of the Sonora desert. No lights on the horizon. If we turned the car lights off it would be dark as a vault. The desert coughed up one star. Heads of horses would jut out in front of the car lights and speed around the windshield like snow flakes only this was a rare dimension moving face, an archetypal horse face. A million years of old faces shining in the night. They were not things that fly by night toward the windshields but horse faces! horse faces! The ghost face of all the dead horses of the parched steppe of time. And time itself frozen into that endless rain of horse faces!. The stars were their bits. The supreme king of all rodents. The Pliocene pony and the horse Pliohippus. There's something weird about those faces. They've done a strange thing in time. They have been around for epochs! Yet they still resemble themselves. We began to philosophize, to think about things. I wonder if there is someone anyone anywhere in this world thinking these thoughts at the same time. Or anyone who has at anytime. I dunno. The wolfman was coming in from L.A. loud and clear. He would yell and howl in the records comin' on the radio. A lone figure on the highway. We stop. A dark earth Mexican peeked in and we talked to him in Spanish. We gave him a ride. He lived on down the road, aje .. aja .. he would gesture (out in there). Out in that dark night somewhere he lived. We came to a village and stopped to have some cerveza.

While we were drinking the owner came over and lit the candles on our table. In a few minutes the lights went out. Our guest told us the man who owned the electricity for the town was going to bed. And when he went to bed he naturally shut off the electricity. We sat there by candlelight, like in a fairy tale. We took him on down the road and he got out and asked us to come to his place and have a beer. There was no light in the night anywhere when we let him out. No signs anywhere, and he said he lived "out there." We shut off the car lights and we couldn't see each other, nothing in the dark. We turned the headlights on and thanked him for the invitation, and went on down the road.

And then by the next dusty road at sunset the senoritas came out on the veranda and swished their full rosy skirts in perfumed lusty swirls. I had my eye on this little brown skinned girl who was just blossoming. She giggled when I winked at her, then she took me by the hand. I went with her to her room and sat down on her cot while she undressed. On her dresser were the icons of her faith and wind up toys and dolls. She wound up this little toy and it walked off the edge of the dresser. She quickly picked it up and put it on top of her dresser and it walked off again. I had to show her how it wound down as I picked it up, and how I could then put it back on the dresser without it walking off.

–Quantos años, tu?

–Doce años.

Ah the smell of cucumber and orange and lemon and leather and flowers in the marketplace. Off to another whorehouse in the battered old taxi honking at pedestrians and pigs tied on to backs of bicycles. A very lovely lady came up to

Bruce at the bar. He tried to get in an aesthetic conversation with her all the while talking about her beauty. Her delicate ankles and brown eyes. He was sure he had discovered a brown princess. How he would like to paint her.

–You fuckee me?

He was embarrassed by the level of conversation as he took her to her room. Before we left Mexico I bought a jar of crisscross bennies to take to drive on. They were real jagged. Bruce had never taken bennies so I told him to take several. He got high and started flashing and talking and drove into the night. I didn't take any and went to sleep in the back seat. I awoke with a sudden jerk, he had put the brakes on because he thought he had seen an altar built in the middle of the highway. I drove some and he talked and talked until his jaws were tired. I got Del Rio on the radio. They were selling Jesus Christ t-shirts and pictures of themselves, and a book they had written which answered such enigmas as whether Jesus Christ had brothers or whether or not it was a sin to own a dog. We came to some kind of inspection station in the mountains. I thought it was for trucks and went on by. A policeman with a machine gun started waving a lantern.

–Shall we stop?

–Better stop.

I backed up the road to the man with the lantern.

–Do you have Merry Christmas for me?

He rubbed his fingers together indicating money. –No Señor nosotros tenemos bastante por gasolina. Bruce told him we just have enough to get to the border.

–All right, maybe next time, o. K.

Bruce took over and drove the rest of the day and all night, singing, talking, chewing. By the time we got to Monterrey his eyes were wide and bloodshot, he had turned green, and his jaws appeared to be swollen. It was just before daylight when we got on a detour. Old Model-T taxicabs bounced along the bumpy dusty streets while their lanterns drew circles in the dawn.

We pulled up to a very funny little kind of soda fountain thing that was right by itself in the dawn. It was a drawing from a comic book. It was blue and red and yellow. We ordered orange juice and this guy showed us his new air rifle with a WWII Air Force insignia on it. I got on a laughing jag and couldn't stop. I left Bruce standing there trying to keep from laughing. He finally asked the guy about his air rifle and he told him it was for shooting rats. By the time we had got to Oklahoma we had turned a fluorescent greenish white like a black light from bennies and road shock. We stopped to get a beer in this joint. All the hot robot tough rods with big bellies stopped dragging Main long enough to come in and throw off bad vibes. We didn't have any vibes. We were stoney and cool. The dogs ran to sniff something from another dimension and couldn't identify any smells so they went about their business.

We were coming back into the Vortex, and I started getting a hollow feeling in the pit of my stomach. We hit that cyclone energy belt where the vibes were strong and always twisting. When the Indians lived there, the sun was God. Now there is an unseen God. This God is everyone's

extreme image of himself as righteousness
personified. And it is O.K. to do wrong if you are
convinced you're right. Great Evangelical giant
took the sun for his own. Right. Righteousness.
Right Wing. What did it all mean? Why were there
rightists and leftists? Right and left. I learned
about this in school. Before that it was just like
the sun. Now right and left like a mysterious
kaleidoscope gradually pulling apart and
going back into another form, always operative
eternal rhythm and pitiful man crudely trying
to duplicate the process with his mechanical-
swastika gears. And that vestigial pineal gland
shaped like a tornado right at the ass of the brain.
Worse than that, the time warp in the Sargasso
Sea! Like curtains closing together and ruffling
back. It was like that time I took those pills J.
had. J. went to the doctor, the shrink, because he
thought he was becoming too homosexual. The
shrink gave him some right-handed pills which
stimulate the right side of the brain. J. layed 'em
onto me, old me, I'd have snake dreams. They
were kind of like psychic energizers but just
energize the right side. I went around cussing
and gritting my teeth, ready to fight anyone or
kick anyone's ass who got in my way. The whole
side of my head felt lopsided, like the right side
was swollen. I had all kinds of snake dreams. Ah
fuck this town and I took off for San Francisco. As
always the end pad of eternity going on out there
in that condemned mess. As always going farther
west and at the end of west where you can't go
any farther, I felt again the feminine suck of San
Francisco. Its energy was all cunt. Suck City. Her
twin peaks bloomed before the skyline. A string

of jewels wound around her body. A seething jeweled vibrating cunt that will always take you in, in, in, into that bottomless cunt pit of eternity and you can't even feel yourself being sucked in until you realize there is very little direction in your own breath. San Francisco, end of the line transgender station, change here for all points. I got off the bus and walked over to Bob's. He had come up from Big Sur and rented a pad in the Haight. He had tried to move a piano in and it fell in the stairwell crashing into the wall. There he left it and played a tune upon entering and leaving. The back side of it made an excellent harp. He was one of the first Big Sur Indians to settle in the Haight. His house was full of visionary paintings in day-glo color and candles, beads, God's eyes. We shot up some smack and listened to Bob's Schubert String Quartet which has an extraordinary sweetness to it. I walked down to Jones St. in the Tenderloin knowing I'd find Betty and Frank down there and no sooner than I got there I saw Frank who was out hustling a few odd jobs.

I got a room in an alcoholic pensioner hotel and watched old men fight. You get old and you never killed, you keep wanting to kill, You haven't had your release, haven't carried out your orders–Cain– from the great apes who learned they can kill because SUBCONSCIOUSLY they are haunted by the strange vapors swirling through the bottomless pit of existence. You get feverish, jumpy.The world is passing you by. There is an imbalance in the chromosomes the antimatter forces are keeping side by side with the life forces. It is a race against time against odds as great in number as all the nameable items in the universe. The need to kill is somehow retained in the masculine ego setup. You've got to apply the personality makeup to the old ape and ass routine. That is also the basis for the swastika. The symbol evolved from an early model of men on their hands and knees with their noses in each others' ass. The easiest place to break individual will and reform it into the precision gear-like mechanical process is, of course, the army. The whole psychological and power set up of war can be seen in the swastika. The mechanism reaches out in right angles like a gear claw. It resembles iron and metal. We feel the residue in the billion little manly decisions we make daily, while we commit genocide, massacre the ghost dancers. Afraid of death, in everyday politeness we open the doors for each other to turn our backsides.

The re-occurring dream of infinity out there on the range where static electricity rumbles on the horizon of beasts like ruffles in the blanket of time. Only the data circuit imprint remains when you close your eyes tightly. Tomorrow slips by until 12,000 days are used up and by then you might be able to see yourself in some unfortunate archetypal mirror-face. The angle of vision will always be off just enough so you don't get a full view of yourself. I wanted to be a mechanical engineer or a musician, anything but this. I am the theory of time in a circus booth, a big mouthed barker wiping the physicist's ass who presides over the re-setting of the official clock in Paris. In olden days Astrologers attended the Ceremony of the Official Re-setting of the Clock. And now physicists attend. They set it ahead about a second, no maybe a fraction of a second, So time had speeded up. I didn't have to read it in this fucking newspaper article. I knew that. Something twitched in the early '60's. Time speeded up, did its little number. Everything speeded up.

A new president. A new frontier. A new decade. Everyone split for SF They were calling me. I went down to Hollywood and stayed in an old apartment building that used to be a five star whorehouse in the '40's. I made a scene there for a while and then went to SF Alan and Bob were there and the older generation that left Wichita years earlier. There was a great sense of freedom in SF I, like a lot of others, threw away all my books and records and began to love, live, and experience instead of defining. I was free! (As free as a Beatles movie it turned out.) But it was good while it lasted. It happened for a good part of a decade. High on the freeways with a swinging feeling above SF's dancing lights, I went over to lower Haight and found Bob. It was afternoon and he was on a mattress on the floor in a dark SF pad. He was watching a T.V. serial, Suzeraine Susan his L.A. debutante was there. She smiled and kissed and took my hand. I went over to find Alan. He was aligned with the soul of those daring young men who left Wichita in the fifties to become SF poets and artists.

After Bob had taken me to North Beach to show me the last of the Beat Generation, we went to Foster Fuds and the Hotel Wentley down in Polk Gulch. So called 'Polk Gulch' because of the rough trade faggot cowboys etc. I found Alan and we talked about putting out a magazine. I would appoint him editor and then proceed to put everything I wanted in it. I hadn't seen Alan since a summer or two ago when he had come back to Wichita. His folks had offered to take him to Europe but he hadn't wanted to go. He just didn't have any reason to go. He would much rather have the conveniences of their house for the summer. Chipmunk had come back with him. She was little, girlish, and could sit and consume all the dope in the world, I think, and never get enough. I had gone to see Alan that summer in Wichita and he was in his flower garden stroking the flowers with his long fingers. He was playing Corelli, softly. He had very psychic hands, beautiful, unfortunate hands suggesting purity. Cupped for innocence. Rare flowers themselves with slender tapering fingers and almond-shaped nails. Hands one instinctively pitied if they have to hold their own in the battle of life. He stroked the plants the same way he would stroke cats. He talked about the strawberries that spring while an ant walked over the cold ground. Alan sat with his music and garden until the leaves fell and then walked into the brisk night, after a day of wheat and side shows and signs pointing toward progress. Inhaling a Kansas Autumn is like tasting a burning sparkler made of virgin's milk. There was Peyote brewing that night. Alan heard a kind of cosmic creak in the atmosphere. He beamed with enlightenment and remarked: "It's Autumn, that's the equinox." He told me he could hear electricity and how there was a difference in the sound of it in different localities. He sat for hours listening to electricity.  He sat all summer and waited for anything, for nothing, and said:

"The hours are not precious.
They are wasted steadfastly and without care,
the day goes like a drop of blood,
the whole world around
the more grooves to lose,
we are found listening at the doors of our tomb."

Now I saw Alan in SF He got me to take some LSD. It wasn't called acid then, and we got it from Sandoz and then Owsley.  Alan said he started tasting himself, and half full of curiosity and regretful torture we broke the Vials and ate the Greenish Pills.  We paraded around the house, innocent and mad.  We giggled and cried and 'eyeball plunged' watching each other change into angels, demons, beasts, old and young. I traced one girl back through her lineage of what it seemed she had been all her ancestry.  Who are you, I would ask, and she would change and change until she disappeared in front of my eyes. I looked at the mirror for a long time and saw myself as both ape and angel, murderer and peacemaker, sometimes pirate and oriental sage. I lay in bed and saw myself change into colors and form flowing around in the covers. The rugs breathed and I was hypnotized like a cat. The toilet stool became a face of a creature gaping. We served a bunch of vegetables and I could feel them like they were a part of my hands. We talked about different levels of meanings.  The world was becoming too impersonal, machine-like. There were magazine articles lying on the floor about the new hallucinogenic drugs. They were becoming popular and hardly a week went by without someone calling attention to them. Everyone kept up with the drug thing. There were those who took it and read the articles on one level, and those who didn't take it who read them on another. Everyone wanted to talk about drugs. It was obvious a big alteration in man's consciousness was coming. I don't think any of us would have suspected the change would come so fast in such quantity. Things were different down in L.A. L.A. was diverse, a real Babylon, a bunch of Wichitas thrown together. Yet it had scenes. Scenes so weird you were always unsure of which movie you may have tripped into. The whole movie thing got to me. I felt like walking up to Mr. Big and say, "Hey! It's me! You'll never meet anyone like me again. I'm Jappa La Torque! I'm C.C. Rider! You may find several of yourself. You'll see many of HIM." Pointing to his secretary. "But you won't see many of me." L.A. was flesh. The tempo was like a bongo drums and surf washing up. The old nutty dried flesh of stars, now characters bleating on the transit system. Had to fight the vampire of L.A. Now I had to see what the vampire of SF was like. Up to Buena Vista Park on acid. Real acid hooking up the whole moon pool of the feminine cunt of SF The lights all beckoning to your own microscopic electrical system. The impulses and desires throbbing. Can't shake it, that same old impulse, and the Breathing Pattern of the sea. Through haggy trees and ghost fog the lights of the Golden Gate make golden the night of beads in the purple haunted fur of Marin forests. Bob had moved down to Big Sur. Susan came up to take acid and we looked out the window of Marion's pad. The night was like a small globe outside the bay windows. The stars were holes worn through thin spots and the outside world leaked through them. A peek through the panty holes into the royal sky splendor. A great liquid energy surged and dripped down into the world like sunlight off tree leaves. And then to the mirror again until its tiny molecules swirled and shone like sequined dreams forevermore. Below was Market St., the large raw gash that ran down from Twin Peaks to the Ferry Building. We knew someone who lived on Clayton. Also someone on Downey, Gough, Polk, Fillmore, Haight, Webster, Oak, Pine, Grant, Green, Mission, and Stanyan. How the patterns of pads would shift around all over these streets for the next ten years. We wandered down into Golden Gate Park high on acid to find a great seer, a great mystic walking down among the wretched, tortured, misled populace of sundry hypocrites. Occasionally I would see someone who was mad or under psychiatric care, and there would be a slight tinge of recognition taking place. Occasionally, too, I would see someone who had the same vibrations, who had the 'awareness' of the hallucinogens. Most of them we called 'heads'. They had a fresh aware look like they had just got out of a hot chemical mineral bath. They glowed. Hippies weren't invented yet.

Alan had seen the futility of drugs and told me that they were just another shortcut.

"I will not walk the road to synthesis again,
I will not take the garish colored pills,

My blood is red and green and proud,
It has its own Mythology."


But he kept on taking everything, searching for something that didn't leave him hung up with just another shuck. Everything turned out to be a shuck. I saw him almost violently mad at the poet McClure because he thought he was shucking him. Alan expected a true honest to God reality somewhere. The more he saw of the ways of the world, the more the shock ate into his face. In Kansas in the 50's he wrote:
"The paths are no longer hidden
and no place dark will hide me.
May I find the Light to face the light
that breaks the light.
And Height to reach the height that crumples height.
And Love to bear the love that stifles Love?"


He always hated his old poems. Bob had inscribed this one on a piece of cardboard and illuminated it. It still hangs on the upstairs wall of the old Gough St. pad.

Alan was as desperate as ever for that immediate glory when he moved in with me on Golden Gate Ave. It was another pee-stained wino pad, smelling of garlic, complete with creepy, marshy, psychedelic, ghost infected woodworks. Alan was sitting down to read THE novel of the time. This was about the 20th time he had read Naked Lunch, unquestionably the greatest underground novel of the decade. In the beginning of the 60s, everyone was reading it. There was almost a conspiracy of silence over it by the mainstream publishers and reviewers. Alan said the Academics and critics were unable to assimilate Burroughs enough to comment on him. Anyway he was THE man in the underground, and that was when the underground was still under. We were talking about this fellow we had heard of who lived in the jungles of South America and could emit ectoplasm from his nose which took on physical forms of priests, tigers, members of his family, etc. The story goes, they sent a team of American scientists and psychiatrists down to study him and they all flipped out and came back crying and babbling. All at once I saw something coming out of Alan's nose! It wasn't snot, it was kind of like a stream of solidified dust particles. "There's something coming out of your nose," I yelled. He threw the book down and jumped up, grabbing at the front of his nose. "You sit over here and read and see if it happens to you," he said. But it never happened again. He laid Naked Lunch down for a while. The doorbell rang. Two dirty crotched girls came by to see us. They stayed for a while, we smoked some grass, they left. Alan said he wished he could have fucked the one he had been seeing. I thought I'd try to cheer him up with a little folk humor but what I said really got to him. He took it seriously and it fucked him up for a few days. He lost sleep over it. It was very hard for Alan to sleep anyway. I asked him very confidentially:

–Do her legs go all the way up to her asshole?

–What do you mean do they go all the way up to her asshole?

–Well! Isn't that the first thing you ask a chick?

Do your legs go all the way up to your asshole?

–Ahh, c'mon, man.

He sat there for a little while making torturous inquisitive faces. He was embarrassed to have to think of it seriously and he didn't want me to know he was taking it seriously.

–You mean there are some girls whose legs go all the way up and some whose don't?

–Of course, that's the first thing you have to find out. Sometimes you can tell just by looking at them with their clothes on. But most of the time you have to find out for yourself.

He became very serious and asked several more questions all about sizes, shapes, specifications, preferences and variations. We discussed the aesthetics of the anatomical structure around a girl's ass and the way some girls' cunts are cupped way down beneath. This type is good to be fucked from the rear. Some cunts stick up; bulge out in the skirt and look very sexy. I suppose it gives the woman the same feeling of dominance as it does the stud on Polk St. who wears a basket. (The pants tight around the cock.) Some chicks like to take it in the ass. Did you ever suck an asshole? It's so nice to suck a clean brown asshole. That should be a song. It's the relaxation it gives them. Nerves and character armor have a direct relationship to the asshole. I went over to M's house the other night. She was practicing asshole therapy. She had her finger up her asshole. I asked her to let me work with her for a while. Now, her legs went all the way up to HER asshole.

–I hear there's a whole (hole) thing going on now in stud bars, sticking your arm or having someone's arm stuck up your asshole. J. said he was propositioned the other night on Market St. So was G. He say's it's big now.

–There was this guy in Wichita who paid kids to shit in his face.

–And all the chili you can eat?

–Buy you chili beans and have you fart in his face. –He was a smart feller.

–er,  fart smeller.

–'The Brown-Out Club.' One thing you have to do to become a member is like go into a big restaurant and pull down your pants and shit on the chair. Or else go up to a big restaurant window when people are dining and pull down your pants and press your ass up to the window.

–Enough of this shit talk. I'm going to bed.

–Do you really think there is a difference between one girl or another as to whether or not her legs go all the way up to her asshole?

–Of course, Alan. Good night.

–Good night.

About the time I got to sleep there was a violent ringing at the door. I suspected it might have been Betty, I hadn't seen her for a while.

–Open this damn door!

–Hello Betty, how are you?

–I want you to meet my friend. We were in the neighborhood and thought we'd drop by and visit my brother.

–I'm busy now, Betty, I have to get up and go to work in the morning.

–That's a hell of a welcome.

She was pretty drunk and had this spade with her.  She wanted to stay but I told her she couldn't and promised I would come see her soon.

The next morning I got up to go to work. I washed the cockroaches out of the coffee pot. Alan was in the front room. He had been awake all night.

–Were you putting me on last night? How can you tell about the legs?

He had thought about it all night long.

–No, Alan, and I wish you'd quit bothering me about it. Just come right out and ask your chick. Better to get it over with.

Below us was the Raped and Strangled Gallery which enjoyed a very brief fame. I had the FUGS play over there the first time they came to SF It was Halloween. Allen G. was there. Jeff Poland came naked with only a placard on him reading: LEGALIZE SODOMY.  Glen was dressed as a cowboy.  We went down to Compton's corner where he had seen this huge queen with a transparent plastic dress on.  She had a bra and slip underneath.  She had a chain leash in her hand, the other end fastened to this guy's neck who was following her on all fours.  Hands and knees.

SF was becoming more and more decadent. There were signs of a vast migration of decaying youth.  Everything on TV., in the News, it all seemed insane. I was still trying to recover from the LSD I had taken many times that year. I was trying to get enough years past so as not to have re-occurring panic reactions and hallucinations and such.  Alan and J. had gone out and picked some poison mushrooms and had eaten them. Alan thought he was part of the roast beef Glen had fixed. J's body had left him he said and he went around in kind of a zombie state.

The next wet, bleak, grey day J. came by and we went up to Bagby. It was a little gold mining town and the fellow who had invented 3D movies was panning gold there. It was one of those strange once-in-a-decade parties where you meet several people who will become intimate friends. It was weird from the start. An old friend and ex-mistress had a hotel and restaurant there. They WERE the town. It was right down in this valley with a river and big hills all around it. The sky was cupped over it. A great orgy.

If things weren't shaky enough in that pisshole on Golden Gate Ave., we had to go and have a fucking earthquake. Alan and I looked at each other, startled. I felt like a gnat riding a vast wave. My sense of gravity was threatened. I felt like a piece of Eskimo sculpture, ready for some giant folds of hands to ferret me from the sick hole of Frisco.

–We're having an earthquake!

–Run to the basement.

–No, that's what you do in a tornado.

–What are you supposed to do in an earthquake?

–Go to the southeast corner of the building.

5.2 on the Richter. We went back upstairs and put on records of Joan Baez, Ray Charles, and Joseph Haydn.

Hallucinogens were coming more and more to the

surface. There was a President, finally, whom you didn't have to feel ashamed of. Alan went back to his brooding, his blond hair standing up like a shock of wheat. He never did figure out

about haircuts. It was just one more unpleasant
task to him to go down to the barber school and
get some Filipino to clip the sides of his head until
they looked shaved. He looked like a scarecrow
in Crimebuster Comics. Like a bowl was put on
top of his head and cut around, like a farm boy
right out of the fields. The funny thing was he
had his hair cut like this all through the hippy
generation, when everyone else was growing
long hair. He looked like a hayseed, and he was
plagued with another problem, that of keeping
his socks from scrunching down inside his shoes.
He always had to stop every few blocks and pull
up his socks. He had a sock problem, either
holes, mismatched or sliding into his shoes. I
tried to reason with him at times why he had this
problem I mean how could anyone be bothered
by such a thing in this day and age? I advised
him to buy better shoes and I think he did. His
blue eyes were always wane, sad, kind, and full
of torture. He had that Hotel Wentley look. His
shoulders were stooped. "The enormous tragedy
of a dream in the peasant's bent shoulders."

–Hey Alan, do you want to be Editor of my
mag?

–Why not?

After we had calmed down from the
earthquake and the hot snot reading the whole
plan began after I told him how beautiful an
old poem of his was. There we sat like recurring
ghosts. Caught in an unknown series of events.
Brought together like faint birth signs.  Alan
hated his poems unless they were "new." He
had a hatred of the past and lived on the verge
of discovery.  Enlightened dreams shot from the

abyss of sanctuary of his soul.

–I think the poem is beautiful.

–You're hung up in the past.

–Then is this mag an organ of the hang-up now in the consciousness?

–If you want to put it in those terms.

–Don't you want the poem published?

–Of course not.

–Why not?

–It's too old. The changes that have happened since make it dated.

–Ez. sd. "Literature is news that stays news."

–I had a very superficial concept of poetry at that time. Art.

–Don't you think you'd be delighted after all these years to write something so pure though naive?

–You can't go back! You know that! I thought we were going to get down to business.

–You're getting defensive.

–You're putting me on the defensive by summing up this situation.

–Listen to this 'Said she from amidst her fragrance/ Now that by sleight/I cast beyond the stars/By this my knee-side pool, the universe.'

–What the hell about it, aren't those absurd lines? The archaic usages alone are to rule it from serious consideration. It's corny academic. It had its day, no need to prolong the agony.

–It's gorgeous poetry, and innocent. Can you recall the image or what it meant?

–Nothing, I, don't know.

A sudden herd of insects ran through his head like someone came home and turned on the lights all at once. A burst of life like near the energy field of Neal the Scorcher. And out in Idaho someone crossing that ancient body of the sea, turns on the car radio and hears wolf man for the first time.

–Do you remember the Clayton St. scene? All that Sandoz and Owsley LSD? Would you do that over again?

–Wouldn't you?

–Could start anyplace, anytime, always the same. –Musta been a bad batch.

–Mike R. said the devil runs his fingers through his brains the way a miser runs his fingers through gold. –Pass the hash pipe.

–I'm tired of using this hand crank.

–I can bust up all the crates in the world.

Alan then busted up some old crates to put into the fireplace. The cold, damp, grey fog rolled in out of the pit of the sea.

–I could bust 'em all and still be left with an empty aspirin bottle and hospital hope. They all tell me to take it to Walgreen's. I get the idea. Sorry to have made such a mess.

–When you were young, did you ever think it would be anything like this?

–Married love, not so passionate but solid and sure, I married death and it's getting pretty old. Dry bitch. Sighs like a gas stove.

–Getting pretty indiscriminate about language.

–Yeah, the whole thing's breaking down. We are now going to examine the parts.

–It seems everyone is taking LSD these days.

–Yeah, it's almost as big as reality.

–When will the Incrimination Requisition come?

–Is that an acceptable fantasy?

–Poetry is just too goddam cute for words.

–We feel each word should be represented, regardless of worth.

–I hate socks!

–Do you see roses?

–Are you putting me on? How come you have to pay a good guy's price and get a bad guy's wages?

–Tom says God is dog.

–Dog spelled backwards.

–Your face looks like Christmas coming.

–There's a huge space vampire holding me for ransom.

–The little Abner bit. Etc. soon drove me to see the streets under the blue sky and orange girders to escape the Irrepressible Crab.

(Always shying away, shifty-eyed at the mention of Burroughs.) Knows a cop when he sees one. Wouldn't you? Past grim-eyed workers punchdrunk under the endless sky of the unbearable tale. (Could you?) Back down the same old hill every time I get there I feel like I've been doing it a thousand years and it makes me feel very tired.

Neal ran in to borrow five dollars to get some speed. Anne was yelling behind him.

–The only thing dirty about me is your cock!

Hair peroxided beyond belief betraying a tamarin archetype, disastrous consciousness shimmering about the eyeballs.

Alan had been taking hallucinogens for two solid years. These were the Kennedy years. The new frontier, etc.

–My life is a speeded up movie on aging. And

here we see the horrible old example. Turned
me down, down down, while the laundromat
went round, round, round. The wrong record
played a million times. Finally it breaks and they
make a new copy. Look straight and keep your
fingers out of your mind while waiting for the
undertaker.

–But no, I had to meddle with the mechanism,
and now, here I am at the wheel of a runaway
truck, with no brakes, steering erratic, leaning
on the horn in last resort eliciting only a feeble
blaaat, brake pedal to floorboard in a terror, one
touch you're not supposed to feel.

The year was 1963, I had moved into the
Gough St. place. Another younger generation
from Kansas had just moved out. Before them
it had been a meth factory. I didn't know until
later the house had an earlier history. Allen
Ginsberg, Neal Cassady, Robert LaVigne, and
Peter Orlovsky had lived there in the fifties. I
had met Neal a year or so earlier when I had my
collage exhibit at the old Batman Gallery. This
house had strange vibrations indeed. It had a
very strange Karma. I was to meet Allen G. there
and watch him exorcize ghosts. The house was
crawling with poltergeists and ghosts. There
was, and still is, the last time I was there, an old
welcome mat at the top of the stairs which has
a swastika superimposed into a Star of David.
I had moved in and painted my room a terrible
gold, red, and black. Both Glen and Dave were
helping me paint. I remember flipping out over
some of Dave's colors. He took over that room
after I left Gough St. and restored it somewhat
and made a very tasty office and Salon for Dave

Haselwood Books. On my dresser were several bottles of Mescaline from Light Laboratories in England. I had a half kilo of strong pot stashed away. There were a few vials of Sandoz LSD around. Young Tom was there who used to wake up in junk nightmares and watch the ghosts parade by. Dennis, a filmmaker from Wichita, was there. Bob had come up from Big Sur. It was going to be one of those San Francisco freak-outs where everyone starts coming together like being drawn into that a psychic whirlpool. That's it, it was just like the twisting vortex energy only it went the other way. "The horn as an emblem of vigor and strength has a masculine character, but at the same time it is a cup, which, as a receptacle, is feminine." The orgastic daisy chain of hang-ups. The strong tornado energy swirling into its own self realization by force and destroying anything that gets in its way, the energy of the white man's God out there on the prairie, the only way to see it. What's a few buffalo and Indians. Gun 'em down at the Ghost Dance. A few Hippies or Gooks or whatever. That was where I came from. Wichita. I can see the whole yin yang galaxy sign right there as two cosmic orgone streams approaching each other from nearly exactly opposite regions of space. The spiral form of conspiracy, the snake eating its own tail when stars came out and the Moon was full. There it gathered together from the underneath ocean into the whirlpool of energy sipped from earth and given to the stars until the riddle of self-awareness vibrated in the night. The other force that simply CONSUMES whatever is in its way, that was San Francisco.

The inverted Vortex. Great numbers of people
would simply get sucked under. They would see
each other and flash some kind of paranoiac
smile and then split to different parts of the
country. And when the Wichita group gathered
in San Francisco a lot went down. There seemed
to be very high arcanum events at the Batman
Gallery and the Gough St. place. Just like the
welcome mat, a cosmic superimposition of
opposing forces. That night I had just taken some
Mescaline on top of horrid paranoia pot. I had
already had visions the weeks before. It was like
the nearer to God you got the nearer to the Devil
also. I had seen the whole Technicolor Tibetan
mysteries flow past. I got higher and higher.
People started coming by. And of all things, the
mad Rocks was coming in from Germany. Two
Cherubim danced in the golden ornate archway.
That was in the same room I had seen the Devil.
I was sleeping then all at once I wake up to this
pulling feeling. I could hardly push myself up,
I pushed myself up with all my might. I looked
over and saw the Devil sitting there in the rocker
plain as day. He was grinning. I can't explain
how he looked because his features were quite
ordinary, like one of those composite everyman
photos. He was dressed conservatively in sport
clothes. But you immediately knew who he was.
I didn't need an introduction. And as I broke
out of the force (like the feel when you hold
two magnets close together), he disappeared.
This time I started being pulled through myself.
Three times I felt it. I ran upstairs to get Glen.
I wanted to have him sample the grass to see if
he would die. I kept shuddering real spaced out,

a case of cosmic horrors. I thought I was dying and I wanted someone else's opinion on it. Glen walked downtown with me. I told him to check me into a hospital and he said we should walk around a bit and maybe call one first. Whenever I passed someone they would point at me. I went into a bar and the first thing someone said is "He looks like a ghost." As we went by people they would make gestures and whisper to each other "tonight." I came down enough to return home and get ready for the party.

A poet who flipped out and got into an ecstatic dance was hung up in astrology and said his house was to rule that night. Astrological battles were nothing new. All the Warlocks and heads were gathering there. The network was buzzing. It was still a fairly open scene. It was the end of the Beat Scene and the beginning of the Hippies. Allen had just arrived in town from India where he had been living since the Beat days. Someone said he was going to be at the party. One of the girls living there had been over to Nevada and brought back some God's Eyes. That was the first appearance of them in the soon to be Hippy Generation. Later the Grateful Dead adopted the God's Eye as their symbol. I heard the doorbell ring and heard some chants and saw Allen's head through the stained glass window. He seemed familiar to the place.

Allen never wasted any time zeroing in. The party was picking up and all sorts of strange people were coming, mostly writers, artists, etc. The earlier poet exile from Wichita, McClure, was there. I did a dance with Phil Whalen. The Wichita gang gave a party for the top guns in town with lots of cosmic double dealings and sneak previews at the super-hip summit conference. I put on Ray Charles and the Clara Ward Singers. Everyone was dancing getting high "out of their brains" as we would say. After Allen had observed the dancers for quite a while and talked with a few people he came through the doorway where I was standing.

–Hello, I'm Allen.

–I'm Charley. You must be some kind of saint or something.

–No. I don't want to be a saint.

The next day or so I went over to Radar's where he was staying. He brought out all kinds of fine food. Caviar, which I couldn't stand. Cheeses and crackers. He showed me letters and galleys of all that enormous amount of work he had done. He almost automatically wanted to go down on me. He asked if I ever had any homosexual relations before and I said all of us guys used to fuck Danny in Wichita. There seemed such a desperate necessity for Allen to have sex with a man. I don't know why, really. As Neal was always saying, "Allen is anal oriented." Anyway it seemed inevitable that poetry was at some time involved in some kind of anal power. He wanted to help Neal write his novel so the plan was to move to Gough St. with Neal and Anne. I had met Neal before and though I had not read much of Kerouac my impression of Neal had stuck. He reminded me of some of the Wichita pill heads I had grown up with. A crazy moving energy. Needless to say Neal was indeed a phenomenon. I'll never forget him unloading his faded c.1939 Pontiac in front of Gough St. The brakes were gone and he wheeled into the driveway and jerked the emergency brake on. He kissed, pinched, and hit Anne, jumped out of the car and picked up a torn cardboard box of belongings with hose and belt hanging out, grabbing them and motioning towards Anne saying "I'm Lash Larue," moving all this time like a jerky speeded-up movie; up the stairs and into the kitchen rolling pot out of an old shoebox, pulling out his pocket watch like the railroad man that he had been, checking the time with worried grey eyes, concerned, soft, and desperate to retain the psychic title of "The Fastest Gun Alive." He ran back through the hall where my chick was perched on a stepladder with no pants on. He immediately paused and started jerking off . . . "just like Playboy magazine" and grabbed Anne and took her in his bedroom and jumped on her fucking away all the time having this heavy Jungian/Reichian conversation about the role of male and female forces. Then he would ask her to hit him and she didn't want to, so he bopped her and fucked her harder and harder with his veins bulging. Allen paused at the door I was peeking through.

–Is he ACTUALLY hitting her?

–Yeah, but not very hard.

I started fucking my chick dog fashion and Allen began to inspect the circumstances intellectually.

–Can you fuck girls from behind?

–Yeah you can fuck them from behind, or anywhere you can.

–In the cunt?

–Yeah, in the cunt, or asshole, or anywhere.

–I'm going to have to try that.

–The asshole is the most mysterious part of our body, in the metaphysical sense, that is.

Meanwhile Neal was deep in his Apache ritual.

The psychological mystique of the asshole. Take for instance working on the dock, all night long there is kind of an asshole comedy of manners of the working class. Those who cannot afford to get "fucked" by the boss, company, Sears, the Government, or whatever, The car dealer who "breaks it off in you" with a bad used car. The whole working shift with men grabbing assholes. All jokes with homosexual reference, combine with an all night effort of proving you're a man and then breaking out into some outlandish fairy dance, husky men shaking their asses, it would put the gay bars downtown to shame. It's a funny thing, though, if you fuck a stud in the ass, (the Italian crew boss broadcast his desire to fuck boys in the ass) or if you let one suck your cock, you weren't considered homosexual and the fact of having what would be defined as homosexual relations wouldn't be considered. Only until you sucked a cock or got fucked in the ass, could you be a homosexual. That's the way it was. So the whole thing was to be on "top." Then you wouldn't be a fag. The Greeks considered it all right to fuck a lad in the ass but if you took it in the ass you lost your honor. Allen would make an intellectual point of fact as he would wipe the crumbs from the table and put the food properly away in a container and then into the refrigerator. A comfortable and Karmically secure thing to do. Something I would see him do over and over again. I felt Allen's approach was always intellectual, he could never shut his mind off, but at the same time his courageous, almost tyrannical headlong exploration into any experience was something to be respected. A good combination too, for his daring maneuvers in the field of legality or politics that make the most astute authorities feel a little threatened. That was Allen, going into the most remote tribes of South America and taking strange drugs (which could have been poison) completely at the mercy of a strange culture and people, alone with their witch doctors, etc. something that our national heroes of OUTER SPACE would probably be most reluctant to do. Here he was lusting trembling after the male cock or ego, always seeming to undermine that type of force which builds empires, enslaves, and dominates at any cost. But falling all over Neal introducing him as his lover as poor Neal was trying to read his work at a poetry reading after Allen had read. What better way to seduce a hostile universe. And then the force sublimated at times to a noble Whitmanesque companion head on breast affection and compassion. Quite a bit different from the screaming Wichita queens I had known. The security of containing another man's seed? It was all too complex for me to try to unravel there on Gough St. Too matter-of-factly and New York business-like for my Midwestern naivete. What seemed the Jewish intellectual mystique or psychic ju-jitsu, pressing for that rational detail until the opponent tried to free himself by any extreme, back to his own personification, completely new to me. I had no racism, at least no acquired racism because I had never known a Jew. Everyone seemed the same to me except for the obvious color of the skin which was different in some races. Other than that, I always looked at the person and knew very little about different races. The whole thing with Allen was to let his opponent rage against him. To draw him out until he fell into his own trap, revealing his own inconsistencies and faults. And then Allen, with sagacity, would be quick to point them out. As far as his love, his desires were quite innocent, and he never really imposed himself on you, and a lot of times suffered lack love himself, while those around him debauched in frequent orgy. However, it seemed with him, a kind of uncomfortable shadowy mysticism around just simple cocksucking and fucking. Though he had his conception about how the world and man were supposed to operate, and an ingenious mind for the practical implementation of these cherished ideals, he was a poor judge of human nature. Or maybe the word "judge" implies something that he rescinded automatically. He seemed totally Eastern in his innocence of judging, selecting, exercising discretion. Maybe it was always an intellectually developed technique to "remain open". In any case, here he was, a remarkable spiritual and reasonable giant vibrating and zapping his analysis of his great insights into events and issues. As far as perceiving personalities, emotions, character (in the sense of total personality) he was a dwarf, or maybe just a provincial New Yorker; when it came to women he was a sucker. You would seldom find him out away from his own ideas, own universe, own poetry, own type, enjoying a person, unless he brought his whole bag of reasoning with him.

Therefore, when it came to new experience, he felt safer in groups, especially groups that had a format, or a group which had been acknowledged in some way by the intellectual establishment (published, recorded, produced, talked about.) You wouldn't find him lost in the anonymous experience of raw literature like a Kafka or a Dostoevski or even Neal for that matter, but there he'd be zeroing in on what was happening in The Underground, Psychedelic, Rock'n'Roll or whatever was big at the moment; except for his visits into other foreign cultures which have always seemed appropriate for writers.

I always felt a little diffident to all that was happening in SF We went over to Sausalito to a party with the Sausalito Intellectuals with a Zen master, painter, I forget his name. The hippies were going to make the Beat Generation look like something very small and out of the past. And they weren't going to look back. The first phase, or Love Generation, was beginning to bloom. I put on my long scarf and psychedelic painted motorcycle helmet and Allen and I took off for the Monterey Jazz Festival. The rest of my costume was a Salvation Army coat, velour pants, and buckled boots. Allen seemed terrified of riding on a motorcycle, but he bravely got on. Then he started chanting and nervously asking questions and making up poems out of signs we were passing. The festival was the big attraction for all the heads. It was one of the first gatherings. Rock'n'Roll still belonged to the middle part of the country, having emerged from Southern Rhythm 'n' Blues, other than in the funky soul of Spade radio stations in SF it was back in the honky-tonks of middle America: Fats Domino, Chuck Berry, Elvis Presley, Buddy Holly, Bill Haley, Joe Turner, Ivory Joe Hunter, Gene Vincent, Jerry Lee Lewis. Back at Gough St. hardly a day would pass that someone wouldn't remark how he or she had seen another 'head' in yet another part of town. They seemed to be getting more and more outrageous, often 'love' would appear on something. Patchen said, "They just keep riding down all the time." Bruce Conner, another Wichita artist, in '61 or '62, had stenciled LOVE on Fell St. in the same huge block letters as Left Turn, Right Turn, etc. We went back to Gough St. Everyone was dancing, smoking, tripping, Ray Charles record playing. This was before the Beatles. Karen had brought Bob Dylan's first record over. Allen hadn't heard him yet so I wanted to play it for him. I remember trying to sell him on the idea that Dylan was a great voice of the times. A few years later Allen played nothing but Dylan records. I was tired of him by then. "And she breaks just like a woman." And Glen asked, "I wonder how he breaks?" Except for some of what I thought were his greatest, I returned to the ones I had grown up listening to. The early Jimmy Rodgers, Hank Williams, Chuck Berry, Bo Diddley, Leadbelly, Odetta.

Everything was saturated with LSD on levels, far out, cosmic, collective, or guilty. I remember showing Allen a quote from Blake I had printed: "Each man is in his specter's power," etc. And I explained to him what it meant. He had one from Shakespeare that ended with something, like, "Whatever strength I have is my own."

The door was open and the tribal poets met. The morning eggs and coffee and Neal rolling a joint. Betty and Frank had hopped a freight to L.A. Everything was moving a little faster it seemed. More of everything disseminating into the culture faster. The whole country started to swing a little. The doors of perception were widening. Jim Morrison was reading Blake and Rimbaud. Though the war was still going on we seemed for once to have a president we didn't have to be ashamed of. Everything was happening. I was sitting around watching TV, enjoying getting blasted. Eating peanut butter. Strangle paste. I would watch the Kennedys go down into Mexico and all the little children reach up for them. I cried at maudlin scenes in movies. Maybe I was just identifying with my own egomania. Maybe it was the peanut butter. We skipped around SF in the parks, over hills, a little band of fools with instant enlightenment. Most of the time just innocently funny on pot or nicely tripped out. We were in the kitchen when Neal and John came running in announcing the Kennedy assassination. We kept watching the whole thing on TV. and Neal and John started asserting their own theories on what was happening and why. Later in the afternoon I quarreled with Ann and we went out and walked around. It was a bleak grey day in SF The wind was blowing trash down the street. There was no noise. A few people were walking but they never looked up. It was cold. There was no hope. Slowly people recovered. I didn't know just how big a shock the Kennedy shot really was. And then not to know why or who. After all the stories were in,

it was still a mystery. People started having their
own theories. A wave of strange things seemed
to come through the news. I could have sworn
somebody on TV. said Johnson had a heart attack
when they told him he was President. I thought
no one wanted to be president or was afraid to. I
fantasized them going all the way down the rank
and file of government officials trying to find
someone to take office, each one feigning illness
or making excuses not to become president.
Everyone became their own detective, trying to
puzzle out what had happened. It seemed like
the end of the whole American system. Why was
I so moved about America? What the hell do
I care if the whole thing comes apart? But yet
everyone began trying to piece it together, or
feeding their own individual madness.  But in
the middle of it all, the Conspiracy, the Karma,
the expanded consciousness, people were trying
to pat it all into shape before the Drunken Spider
spun its web. It was increasingly obvious that the
sum total of our culture was quite mad. Things
kept getting more unbelievable and crazier.
Allen wrote a poem about that Historic Day. He
thought that the Warren Report would come up
with the most reasonable explanations.  I think
it got to the point where one had to believe the
Warren Report just to quit thinking about what
had happened. It seemed like some super cosmic
destiny pattern that involved the neuroses of
the whole country. Each one could go into his
own paranoiac fantasy. And there were more
complicated facts being added all the time
to feed the theories. How could you keep it all
together? Might as well accept the Report. What

else were you going to do? We had Thanksgiving
dinner at Gough St. Frank had hopped a freight
up there and we had a huge dinner in the dining
room around the big round table. Frank was
coming off a drunk he and Betty had got on in
L.A. He was straightening out and was amused
by Neal's antics. Years later he would tell Neal
anecdotes to the guys on the dock. After a while
the scene split up. I went to Tucson to visit Bruce
and took Ann back to Wichita for a while, I bought
an old Buick in Tucson. Going back into that
Vortex was always an emotional drain. I started
feeling empty in the gut when I got to the Outer
Extremity of the Vortex. I felt the vast loneliness
of space. I felt like a bug crawling along the floor.
I felt the warm wind come across the prairie. I
saw whole skies light up with lightning. And the
distant roar of thunder, crack and roll as if the
world was coming apart. I had not heard thunder
all the time I was in SF Only once did it thunder
all the time I was in SF Residents of Daly City ran
out to see what was happening, some of them
had never heard it before. That's what's wrong
with San Francisco poetry–I thought to myself–
no thunder. I was glad to leave San Francisco. I
wanted to be in seasons again. In real weather.
I got tired of the same old climate there. But
Wichita was the same old shit. Gawky little
people. Busybodies. The Nuevo Rich descendants
of hardy European Stock. They had a little now.
Good home. Good car. A lawn. A power mower.
They weren't about to jeopardize that. Some had
come out of hovels in the South. They finally
made it when they could dine in Clean Plastic
restaurants. It didn't matter how awful the food

was just so long as it was a clean place. Farmers
and aircraft workers would take their families
into these god awful big chain restaurants off the
new interstates. The management knew these
suckers well. Instead of a good meal they would
serve the most horrid plastic food imaginable.
The customers came in in their starchy shirts
and ties and peeled heads. How nice to step in a
thick carpet and have piped in music and clean
vinyl chairs and paper-meringue pies. For these
pleasures they paid well and paid most of the
taxes in the U.S. They bought on time and paid
their interest, They carried the country with the
money from their lowly wages and never knew
the difference, nor probably cared, because they
were loyal and just let someone try to tell them
about how mankind could better his lot and they
would take it straight to God, to Mother, and the
Flag. It seemed I had to be constantly talking
about Religion or about Communism every time
I went back to Wichita.

Not only did it seem I had to converse on
just two subjects, I had to preface my positions
with all kinds of references which I thought
were common knowledge. In Wichita it was
rare to meet someone who had read a book.
It took so much explaining just to be able to
make a rational statement. It was the same at
the University. Always trying to keep up with
Jones U. Never really developing its own talent.
I got in the old Buick and drove to N.Y. The East
Village was just happening. Ed and Allen took me
around to poetry readings to meet people. I felt
very paranoid about everything and took off for
San Francisco and then up to Alaska. The same

old magical feeling of joy arose when I saw SF all lit up. The golden lights across the Bay Bridge and the Golden Gate. I felt as free as a teeny-bopper. I wasn't there long until it seemed as if certain psychic elements in SF started forming together in the same old protoplasmic pool. Each archetypal essence paraded itself carrying its own vestige its own reality root. The clairvoyant call sounded into familiar reality clusters. I was beginning to feel old. It seemed like between 25 and 30 I became more aware of death. It was always around. I went down to North Beach to Vesuvio's and watched the old Bohemians tilt wine glasses with fingers laden with big arty silver rings. I saw old Beatniks who had long since gotten a job, trimmed their mustaches and hair and bought a sports car. Everyone was still talking about hallucinogens. I quit taking them. I thought that either the racial consciousness was expanded enough so that there were no more great gulfs and chasms to explore, or the new acid was not as powerful as the old, to judge it one would have to listen to a million trips or take them or maybe it was possible to stretch oneself over many reality patterns thus coming back to reality, or nature itself and its trillion manifestations. Anyway I was tired of it. I went over to Michael's and he was tired of talking about it too but he couldn't resist trying to stay on the bandwagon when the new crops arrived. He even set himself up as "guide" to the Haight Ashbury. The wind of the Haight was in the air. Another Michael, a painter who used to be on the street in North Beach in his Jag every night was to ask Leland, "Which way is Haight and Ashbury?" He set up shop there next day and became a popular guru and spokesman for the scene. Bob had left the Haight. He couldn't survive in the city. He would always go back to the Sur. He had moved from the place where the piano was stuck in the stairway crashed to its side, not until he invented several compositions for the strings in back of the piano. Bob had painted many rooms in old Victorian pads and had openings of 'rooms'. He was one of the first Big Sur Indians with a headband and beads and LOVE painted on his truck. He set the style for a generation. Rocks and I drove down to Half Moon Bay to see him. He had a room out in back of his house that overlooked the ocean. It was covered with paint. Some splashed, some spilled, and some worked into alchemical and metaphysical designs and figures. He said Alan had been by and came around to the room just as the lights went out. Bob had been trying to get off junk as the lights went out. There he was groping around in this black nightmare and when the lights went back on again he said Alan was standing in the doorway with large fangs and blood dripping off them. There was some very strong hash and some junk down there and Rocks and I went out to score some. Bob was becoming very good on the cello. He played it sweetly like his record of pure junky sweetness, the Schubert String Quartet. Rocks and I drove back up the coast highway toward SF We began hallucinating wildly. We would change into several different people and at the same time it seemed we were on a film that jerked a little at every still until it almost stopped in a 'reality still'. At that point

Rocks turned into an old lady and he said I turned into Henri Fabre, the fellow who wrote about insects. I had been reading a book of his Glen turned me onto. All about experiments with these poor silkworms which he had crawling around the edge of a vase, each one clinging to the thread, their guiding light, their hope, like we cling to our intelligence. To conduct an experiment the author had connected the ends of the thread and thus the worms crawled around and around unto their doom. A man-god had linked the ends of their intelligence, their psyche, "Will the circle be unbroken, bye and bye Lord, bye and bye." What if some God had linked our intelligence in a similar fashion? What if there is no hope and all man does is go around and around for millions of years, doing the same thing, committing the same atrocities, the same mistakes, eternally trapped in the same paradox of death. Killing over any threat. Groping around in the dark eons of time. Nothing but a thread of light and a leader to guide them. That's what our country tis of thee is based upon, a leader and the light. I saw the light. Rocks' face turned towards me in the still; changing into a horrid teenager in Colorado driving his car over his Fraternity brothers' lawns. Hating them and himself. Driving, driving across that insect nightmare night of the plains speeding toward nowhere. And now here we were speeding up the coast highway. A huge choir appeared all along the mountains laced in and out of the trees and slopes and valleys.

–Roll the window up. Quick!
–It's no use I can still hear it.

The Angelic music grew louder. Like Haydn. A mass. Vivaldi.

    –The car is upside down!

    –We're floating out over the Pacific!

We got back to the outskirts of SF and Rocks bought some wine.

    –Man if I ever come down I ain't gonna never take nothin' again.

He started hitting ninety into the curves of the SF skyways which are pretty tight anyway and designed for speed. The back end of the car started bouncing sideways as Rocks threw it into second. The floor under the clutch pedal had been stomped through and you could see the pavement as his mind flashed to the race track in Germany. His eyes were big and peered into a shriek. He looked the same as that time he had come by the hotel with Neal and two chicks in a VW on speed and lush, wearing headbands. Both having a thing about driving, talking about racetracks. The mad VW winding down the hill. Neal's arms out the window waving. Rocks gesturing wildly in the night. Rocks' chick driving. Neither Neal nor Rocks at the wheel. It was like approaching the Indianapolis 500 with a go-cart. This male driver energy being chauffeured around SF in a VW.

Though Rocks always had a different chick, he always complained he wasn't getting enough. I decided one day to go to an introduction service with him to see what kind of stranger worlds we could get into. There was this one operated by a nice old Jewish lady Rocks got all hung up about wanting to fuck. For it didn't matter what or who. Each person was another lifetime a whole entirely different world that Rocks could dip his tongue into and eat every last drop out of the pussy. What is life anyway, flying past, death racing toward you. What can you do but search for hiding places and little crevices to enter and stay a while. Fresh reality. Hoping always for something fresh enough to last. But knowing always it goes like the flower. Death lets no love bloom for long. Got a debt to pay. Remember? Racing from one house to the next. Speed, booze, or pot, or anything to take it all away for one instant. We sat in the office of the introduction service.

–What are your hobbies?

–Stamp collecting.

(Stamp collecting?) I just looked down at the floor. No I can't break up laughing now I'll blow the whole thing. What the hell does he mean "stamp collecting" I had never known him to have a stamp collection. Here I am all blasted away, trying to go through this interview, and he comes up with stamp collecting. My face grew red and I acted like I was yawning so I wouldn't crack up in laughter. Oh shit now she's going to think we're some kind of idiots. The pressure mounts. I want to run out. I have to stay and make a proper impression to get one of her girls. I can't even give her straight answers. Maybe she thinks I'm retarded. Rocks gets mad and indignant about my reaction to his stamp collecting. He looked at me in his proper insurance salesman best.

–Yes, STAMP COLLECTING. I have been collecting stamps for years. I have one of the most complete stamp collections around. I haven't kept up with it much these past years, however, but I always like stamps. That and classical music.

There he sat with all the character of a kaleidoscope. The more bizarre his episodes the more defensive and serious he got about them. All this shit he had done. Even the Army was embarrassed about him. Even THEY didn't even know what to do with him. Kept sending him into the most remote spots available. They tried to forget he was part of them. They never got him for going AWOL because they never wanted to admit he was in the Army. He went anywhere in Europe whenever he wanted. And if you have the potential to fuck up the U.S. Army, you gotta be a Fuck-up.

-Were you ever in the service?

-Yes, I served in Europe.

I had seen him demonstrate what he would do if they ever called him back. It was eating anything from a bowl of sugar to going out on the firing range and getting a gun and going berserk with it. The interview was over, and I made some excuse to come back later. Rocks had gotten a list of names and dates from her and was about to set out with them. More emotional than the average guy could ever be but completely unemotional toward the task that lay ahead. That is, getting in some girl's cunt. If he did let himself get caught up in the conflict of life the impact with which he was operating would completely wipe him out. He could be deeply in and out of love as quickly as the telephone poles going past the car window. Or the endless movie with the scene in another bar or time or country or city or story or love. Like the window of eternity going past the telephone pole. The faster you went the faster they would fly by. There was no escaping. Rocks picked up his date the next night and started in the whole thing. A few bars. Maybe a drive to Sausalito.

–I hope my driving doesn't scare you.

–Oh no, not at all.

–Do you get scared in cars.

–No, nothing can scare me.

–Really?

–No. You can't scare me with your driving.

–I bet I can, just a little bit.

As the poor girl made the mistake of presenting a challenge, Rocks' brains flashed on and off like a distant pin-ball machine in some home town drug store. His eyes flashed and his mind scanned the race track in Germany. He went up near Jones St. to find the steepest hill in SF Up he went as fast as he could go and then over the top screeching sideways, smashing into parked cars. The poor girl went to the hospital with some minor injuries and Rocks went back to the introduction service to get another date for the next night.

Were the girls just another soul crab to open and dig the meat out of? No. They were in fact an open door into the eternity of the opposite force. Rocks took the girl some flowers. The agency finally dropped him. He tried to fuck the old Jewish lady while she was arranging dates for him. He rented a car for a while and appeared with a one-eyed girl. One night he had a vision about his wife in Germany. He immediately got on the phone and called her after not being in touch with her for over ten years or so. He had telephone operators all over Germany trying to locate her. He laid some weird emergency story on them. They finally sent out messengers on bicycles to try to find her. After about $90 in calls and a day and a night on the phone he located her and split to Germany again. Though he didn't speak German fluently he did manage to get a job in a camera factory and worked there while she convalesced in the sanatorium in which she was found. He then made arrangements to bring her back to the States.

We went walking down to the Tenderloin and saw Frank on the corner of Turk and Jones. He told me where he and Betty were staying. They staked me to room rent and I moved in a dingy hotel on Turk St. in a room adjoining theirs. Betty was always pleased to have one of the family around. One who could accept her and how she lived. Next door lived a pensioner who thought he was captain of a ship and talked into his tape recorder and played it back to himself. "I don't care how much money you have, I'M captain of this ship." All day long he played it back. The dingy Hotel Nut House. I went downstairs and sat in the lobby next to this woman. She had a face like a rabbit and kept twitching her nose. Every once in a while she would break out laughing. The desk clerk would look up. I started thinking about just laughing and laughing. There was nothing to laugh at but perhaps something to laugh about. Perhaps the center of the Universe is laughter. Was it a mad joke or pure Joy? I didn't know but I laughed anyway. She stopped laughing and the desk clerk looked up at me next. She had this

little wad of paper she would roll between her
fingers. I would see her doing this for hours and
days on end. While I was sitting next to her she
dropped the wad of paper on the floor and dived
after it. She moved so quickly I thought she had
dropped some fire off her cigarette or something
so there I was down on the floor helping her
retrieve her little wad of paper. I went back up to
the room and thought about getting a job. Betty
was on a drunk and wanted me and Rocks to take
her to the bus station.

–I'm leaving this muthafuckin' town, I'm going
to Alaska.

She was in really bad shape by the time we got
to the station. She had been on one for days and
it didn't look like she could get off. I had been
going to A.A. meetings with them but that only
lasted for a while. Rocks and I suggested taking
her to a hospital and she blew up. She went over
to her locker and started throwing things at us,
cussing and screaming. She threw her boots
at me and I ducked into a phone booth. Rocks
ran into a corner dodging her toiletries. She
threw everything she could get her hands on
and soon all her belongings were all over the SF
bus depot. People walked around them ducking
with that "only in San Francisco" look. Rocks
and I just left her there, poor kid, but she was
on the warpath and there was nothing we could
do except get out of her way. I moved into the
old Oak St. mansion which had belonged to the
Fleishhaker family at one time. There were two
old bald landladies who went about their daily
routines quite unperturbed that the old place
had housed one of the most notorious open

dope scenes in SF for many years. It was the forerunner of the crash pad. It still had gas lights in the living room. Betty banged on the door. She was drunk and had a spade trick with her. I told her she couldn't stay unless she got rid of her trick and bottle.

–You little muthafuckin beatnik. I can't even visit you. My own brother!

She went down the stairs cussing. I sat down in the kitchen and started reading a book. The pot smoke thickened in the hallway. I heard the front door open. Two men came up the stairs. The first one asked me if they could come through the room to get up on the roof. I didn't like the incorrect grin in his eyes. I knew they were cops. They said they were looking for a robber. I told them to go ahead, and continued reading In Search of the Miraculous and smoking my joint. They came back through the kitchen and thanked me.

–You're welcome. I GUESS.

Betty came back to sober up. She and Frank rented a room at the Oak St. mansion. We put some vegetable stew together. Betty had a black eye and her face was bruised.

–Who are those nuts next door?

–Just some kids dealing acid and speed.

–This little nut was in here visiting us the other day. She had this cat in her arms kissing it. The cops came looking for someone next door. They came over here to ask her about them and her cat ran out the window. She ran out after it. We were on the second story and there's nothing outside. The cops didn't even go look out the window. They just left. The little nut, she just went out the window and vanished.

–She was probably some kind of ghost.

–And that door over there it all of a sudden bangs wide open. Even when it's locked.

–Poltergeist. I had the same trouble. Thought I was going nuts.

–You ought to go to a shrink.

–You too.

–I'm not going to one of those jerk muthafuckers. They tried to get me to see one when I was in the joint. They're all a bunch of jerks.

–Complete assholes.

–They didn't have them before the war like they do now. You never heard anything about them then. The war made 'em. That's what everyone said. Better study to be psychiatrists. Now they're all over. The fuckin' war made them. We didn't have them before the war. They're all a bunch of pricks. If it wasn't for the fuckin' war that made everyone nuts, we wouldn't have them.

–Little pricks driving around in their red sports cars.

–Wha'd you do in Tucson?

–I went to see a friend of mine: Bruce. He showed me the old section of town where the whores were. I fucked this one. The Creature from the Black Lagoon. I never did know what she looked like exactly. She took me out behind a building and I fucked her standing up. For $5.00. It was the whole setting. Sinful red lights. Evil blue neon in the red dusk. Hickory smell and wine in the dark stench of night. The atmosphere itself made me lustful. I took my chick back and we went down the street where the brown women sat in unpainted chairs tilted against adobe walls.

–Hello.

–Hello.

–Can we go inside with you?

–You want a date?

–Yeah.

–What about her?

–She can come too. It's all right.

–Oh, My!

We went inside and she wet a towel. My chick helped her undress. She had full brown tits and round stomach that curved around to her muscular thighs which were firmly stacked into neat jutting buttocks. We started running our hands around in the shiny black coarse hair of her snatch. Then we all sucked each other off.

-Do you remember that time we were working on the Dalles Dam in Oregon? Betty and I went over on the Washington side to see a whorehouse she had known about. We drove up this little winding road and came to a hilltop where an old burned out foundation was. (There were little lines of rubble indicating the space of rectangular rooms where burned up emotion sped away on the charred remains of cots into which the wind played as it raced over the hill touching the wildflowers and down the valley to where the wild rapids roared into Portland to the calm Pacific. A lamb played in the chilly breeze the grass was yellow and huge clouds puffed in the sky. It's as if we were somewhere we'd been before, or not been; or will be again, or never. While it lasted maybe it's the pleasure of life itself. And only life is remembered. Life is pure joy. A release. Freedom from all gravity and time. While it lasted each event seemed like the complete emotion. A long story unwinding without beginning or end. No more emotion. The memory is not easily felt. The conflicts were trivial crises of unaccountable billions that make up a routine day. And then the years speed by. It was only yesterday when, . It is hardly worth the trouble to think about it. The days screeched by like the broken record of time. What is happening? I am here now.  Someday I won't be here. Where will I be? Me. I'm hiding behind everything in the world. The real me is hiding. Knowing that someday I won't be here. Where will I be? Is that the whole history of me? The sum total.  Driving from town to town. What is this whole thing? Anyway? The years passing. Wrinkles and pot bellies.  What to do? Where to go? Where can I wait out the Reality Nausea? The Young Flowers, they have a choice. Be cut down and take their chances being planted in someone else's suburban rose garden every summer, or roll around, blow around with the wind, planting their seeds where the wildflowers bloom. Drifting around in raw emotion before it becomes a story, fantasy's companion, where pure fiction reigns, and desire is spent like hot billionaire come, golden time is thrown away, forever spent for pure drama, more time spent than graft will ever accomplish, more freedom than any government could buy with all its tonnage of murdered flesh, the life force being beautifully alive with no thought of recompense, where dreamers go and novelists are not allowed.)

   –Remember Little TOOT?

–The little boat I lived in on the Columbia River? I didn't have a place to live until payday so I went out on this boat and camped. I got up every morning and went to work on those big air drills drilling all day into rock. Wagon drills they called them. They were mounted on wheels and pounded and drilled holes in the side of the mountain either to put re-enforcing steel in or to put dynamite in. They were developed from the steam drill, I guess. The one that replaced the hammer of John Henry.

–Remember we went down to that joint in Portland?

–And that real ebony gal in a green dress took you home?

–What ever happened that night?

–I just went home and stayed with her. She was real nice. Tall lanky and warm. Shiny black, beautiful face like an African Zulu princess. We ate some baloney she had. When we got in bed she took hold of my cock and said, "My, you ain't no baby."

–That reminds me of a trick I had up in Miles City. He was an old bachelor and took out this neatly folded hanky he had cut a hole in and hemmed up. He put his prick through it when he fucked so he wouldn't catch the crabs.

–Remember that joint in Bend, Oregon. All the girls lined up in their little trick suits.

–I had one trick who popped his nuts before he got it in.

The sun glistened on the ancient green plants that surrounded the old Oak St. mansion. Frank had put on some vegetable stew. Neal the scorcher came by and started talking about the horse races. I had been reading a book about the outlaws of the old west. I introduced him to Betty. I was telling Neal I had found a picture of Butch Cassidy and the caption under it was "top gun of the wild bunch". All the literary people referred to Neal as the top gun or fastest gun. Big names were referred to as big guns. In Neal's case it was that he was the fastest free word associator around. Sometimes people would come around and 'draw on him' or try to out-associate him in a conversation. Sometimes his fantastic ability got to be a drag because he used it in a defensive way. I was telling him Butch Cassidy had his same archetypal features, and that towards the end of his career he settled around Denver. Neal was from Denver. He never cracked to my trying to place him as Butch Cassidy's grandson. I don't know how that would fit in with the medium's stories of his past lives which were on the tapes he carried around. He sometimes played them while he was talking to and fucking Anne. Neal had gotten a job down near the Tenderloin at a tire changing place. He worked so fast they finally had to let him go because the other men wouldn't have anything to do. As they say in Texas, "he wuz so busy, you'd think he wuz twins." I drove in one time and he changed two tires in between checking the air in mine meanwhile giving me the full advice of all the tire pressure manuals and road conditions and load and how it related to tire pressure. Zip, zip and he was filling up the tires. Zip, and he was back taking one off the rim, introducing me to all his workers who already knew he was some kind of incredible person. Though all sorts of weird

people came by to see him there, he was in solid
and had captivated the attention and respect of
his coworkers. They couldn't put down anyone
who outworked them. Then Anne came by and
he immediately got into a knockdown and drag-
out argument which provided the afternoon's
entertainment. I think it was Kesey who, a few
years later, had the brilliant idea of renting the
Longshoreman's Hall and billing Neal & Anne in
their great performance. And it turned out to be
the invention of mix media dances. Betty and
Frank went on a drunk.

For self preservation, I had to move out of the
Oak St. mansion. I went back to Wichita for a
while. It seemed everyone had gone back for a
visit. Moody's Skidrow Beanery was in its prime.
Down among the day-old doughnuts and rooms
full of organs, dirt, books, coffee, monkeys,
bums, juke box, paintings, popsicle trucks, were
two managers from New Orleans. It was kind
of a bums' version of a coffee house. The police
were always trying to close it down. Ike and
Chloe opened a store next door to the Gypsies.
I got Glen real blasted and took him down in
the Skidrow Beanery catacombs. "Man, it's too
much," he said. Moody finally had to close up.
Later Moody was to have "The Great Wichita Be-
In". The news photographer took the picture.
About a dozen people went out to the baseball
stadium where Moody put it on. They sat there
on the benches saying "Where's the be-in? Or
what's a be-in? Or what are we supposed to be
in?" Wichita was kind of like San Francisco had
been in its dependency on culture from N.Y.
or Europe. San Francisco finally did a thing of

its own. But Wichita was always a few years in waiting to get what was happening. Instead of making it themselves, they depended upon what came from the coasts; except for the 'folk artists'. At the same time, though, being isolated from what was happening, you weren't so saturated and could develop original work. And if you stayed in Wichita and persisted in your enjoyment of country music there would come a time when it would be in vogue. About two weeks was all I could stand being in the Vortex now. All kinds of subtle little things started mounting up into my overworked paranoia. Dave and I were driving back to SF Pat, a painter who painted monkeys and birds and lived in some kind of Dream State, wanted to ride back with us. We were leaving from Crandal's place where her folks brought her and said, "This is Pat. I hope you can do something with her." Driving back across Utah I began to get tired. I asked Pat if she could drive. She hadn't said much all the way and kind of sing-songed dreamily:

–Yeeaahh.

–Do you have a driver's license?

–Yeeaah.

–Well I'm going to hop in the back seat. You take it for a while. Dave sat up front with her, and he and I smoked a joint. He was in his Za Zen trance looking out over the vast nautical ruins of Utah. Pat wound up and down the mountain roads. I noticed that every time she came to a curve she would drive way over to the far side of the road off onto the shoulder of the oncoming lane above the great cliffs. Then she would jerk her head to the right and then just in time jerk the steering wheel to the right and come back safely to the right side of the road. At every curve she would go through this procedure. Always the same. Meander over near the edge, jerk her head, and then turn the car back. Those cliffs were getting deeper and deeper. I was completely blasted and was thinking what in the fucking hell is going on? I tried to ask Dave through a series of glances to kind of see if he could interpret the whole thing and maybe say something. But he would look out over space with his cosmic Za Zen smile beautiful. He would have probably rather let us plummet to our death in the deep ravines than say something that he thought a Za Zen wasn't supposed to say. I knew I couldn't rely on him for any fucking help.

–Hey, ah, Pat, would you mind pulling over down here. I have to take a piss.

–o. K.

–I might as well drive into the next town. We can stop there and eat. Are you guys getting hungry?

–Yeeaah.

–I could use a little food.

Actually we had a pot starvation going and Dave and I couldn't wait until we got somewhere to scarf; Pat didn't smoke any pot. While our food was being prepared I thought I'd mention the drive to see if Pat would volunteer any reasons for her peculiar driving patterns.

–Boy! That was quite a road over the mountains. Silence.

–Ah Pat. I was wondering why you went over to the far side of the road on those curves and then suddenly turned back to the other side.

–I was hearing voices.

–Oh.

–How about some coffee, Dave?

–Yeah, let's have some coffee.

All during the meal I kept remembering that melodic tone when she answered. It was almost sing song. "I was- hearing-voices." She stayed at Gough St. for a while and seemed to remain completely oblivious to anything that was going on. She married Dave, a poet who danced at the big party that night. He was a kind of collector. They moved over towards the Fillmore in one of SF's most decrepit buildings where you could rent a 7-plus room flat for $60 per month (near the Greta Garbo Hotel). She painted and he collected (very odd things) and wrote poetry. We rolled into SF just as the old Ford was giving out. It seemed good to be home. The only place I could call home. It was home to everyone who had no other place to go. Betty, Frank, Neal. San Francisco had that thing about it. It was the great foster mother city. She always opened her beautiful hole right up. And sometimes her bosom. I went back over to the Oak St. mansion to see Alan. Some chick had come over to see him because she liked the sound of his name on the door. She rang, and came upstairs and got in bed with him. She was one of the most far out chicks I'd ever seen. She looked like she had been many times reincarnated and her face was plastic surgery attached to ancient mummy bones. She was quite good looking, though. Kind of looked like a drag queen. She was a female counterpart of Neal when it came to association in all directions at once. Meanwhile zapping everyone with rays from her magic ring. Kassandra was from another world and came over here to Alan's to live.

–I haven't been to bed for 2000 years. My face ran when I burned it in the mirror. I gave up my arms when I was robbed by the Arabs. You like my ring?

–ZZZAAAPP, zap, zap. I came to this white bastard's house, blond. Blue eyes.

She seemed to be part Spanish. Her father was Spanish. And she said she started making it with him when she was a child. She spoke jive talk.

–I just fell off five stories in Chinatown, with my Roman lover. While the spirit war was going on in the South. I tricked this chump from commercial chicken shit town, black Puerto Rican, just met the punk, can't stand him, drank Ancient Age, I was bruised from head to foot, went to Reno, I was Regina and the Taurians cleared the street. Then back to the record shop where I live on Wednesdays this fuckin' high yellow, he knows voodoo, and all his fuckin' paintings of clowns crying, I tore them up, the Martian burn. He wanted to live on my pussy, he say, 'get up and wash.' MUTHERFUCKER, suck it funky! He wore eight pairs of pajamas, sucked off my pussy and I bled all over him, ain't that cold? I burned my ovaries with a sunlamp up in that room, with tricks from the convention. Detectives came up, say I didn't have enough luggage, shavin' kit with razor and dope. Dick Dog Taurus pulled out his prick, looked like leprosy, white scaly scabs I had to put 5,000 band-aids on. Found this chick, she tried to finger fuck me for the first time, K Y on night stand, all the fags got a key to the kitchen.

Jumped on my lover's chest with spikes on, he took me to the King Tut exhibition, marks up and down arm, from the crystal meth palace.

The Goldwater primary! The TV. was on covering the events at the Cow Palace. There were all sorts of crazy commentaries that accompany the political circus and it seemed all the more crazy to me in my own mental state. To see all the pot bellied mama-men crewcut fat-ass-pink cowboy shirt and hat and all the little piggy cheerleaders too much. Goldwater had every intellectual terrified. I was terrified. I had to be. But yet down deep I secretly admired some of Goldwater's views. He seemed to be honest. At least he would have DONE something that the Democrats could oppose and then get back into power instead of them just petering out, disintegrating by way of their own deeds. I think the British wanted to see Goldwater in. I don't know why. I suppose he would put on a better show for them. But I would have never voted for him. It was against my nature. Everything I stood for. Or didn't stand for. How could I have voted for him? I would always be suspected of being some kind of cop. Even though I was secretly tired of the Intellectuals, It was funny about Neal. His archetypal features resembled Goldwater. Same kind of morphology, I was at one of those weird Batman Gallery openings when I saw Neal with some other people who came by to score some dope from some of the people in the gallery. They were all dressed in Goldwater campaign paraphernalia, the Red Garter straw hat bow tie thing with Goldwater buttons pinned all over them. Flags and canes and banners. Neal was quite an attraction at the opening. The intellectuals, art patrons, and heads all thought it was a great put-on, I'm sure, but no one would think it was anything but a put-on. No one wanted to ask him about his politics. He went to the convention. Had a great time

Let's all get out of our shells and bravely venture forth and have a good time in the other camp. Unless it's incriminating, it must be a joke. But then the war goes on year after year after year. We hear the statistics on TV. We see a few feet of war film. The wrong war. We didn't want that entertainment. It costs more to produce those War Games in Vietnam than it costs to care for humanity itself, the flesh itself taken out of God's body weighs the earth down forever, down in its predatory hell where the reptile's face hides innocently behind the brows of your good neighbor. Or neighboring countries or worlds. Not until Mars or Venus close together will the dimensions of the final star be completed. And near the TV. the beer goes flat while in Vietnam children play along the dusty road of death, unable to comprehend the sound of planes above them. A death spraying helicopter hovers above them while they play with sticks and look through the rubble for food. A crying infant cannot know what comes from those things in the sky. Why should it happen? What kind of war is this? Mad America wouldn't listen. Surrounded the Ghost Dance and opened fire on people who were different. They cannot explain to themselves what war is. Tom, bleeding, crying hysterically behind the burning huts. A baby crawls into the flames and burns. Her father's ears were cut off to make a GI's love beads. Her brother's penis cut off and left sticking in his mouth. Primitive symbols of an unknown hell. In the helicopter one pilot smoked a cigar and the other secured his horn rimmed glasses.

I got sick of California and went back to Wichita. I was engaged in this inevitable conversation about Christ and I was talking about how Christ must have felt on the cross. Questioning God himself. Into all the Christ Magic Universe and reality walked a cat. I had always got along with animals. I even passed the monkey test with Radar's monkey. I always like cats and dogs or any animal. But, this cat I knew something was wrong the minute I saw it. Its fur was full of brambles and that was a bad sign. Also it looked tormented. It came straight for me and I froze. For some uncanny reason I didn't want it to touch me. It came over and brushed against my right foot and ran out the door. I ran after it trying to get the others to touch it too. We couldn't catch it. The next thing I did was get on a skateboard and fell off and broke my right ankle. I had to have surgery at the hospital. The doctor had to put two pins in my ankle bone to hold it together. It turns out the cat also had broken its right leg and had to have two pins in it. I was relating this story to the pot smoking sheriff minister at a party one night. I described the cat to him and he said he had a cat like that and that he had been on mescaline one time and had put the devil in his cat which later ran away. I was laid up in Wichita with a cast on and Allen called and said he was coming to visit the Vortex and to wait around. He called me when he got in

town and I went down to Fairland's Cafe to meet
him. G. an old time Greek gangster had already
befriended him. We left the Chinese cafe and
walked down Broadway. Allen, Peter, Julius and
myself. Allen said, "Well here I am in Wichita,
B'Gosh." What followed then was the usual
account of police and poetry action. We gave a
reading down at Moody's Skid Row Beanery. The
rainmaker had come to town. Curious students
thronged around him. Teenagers stopped
dragging Douglas Ave. long enough to note the
hairy bard. The John Birchers grew indignant
and watched him and waited for him to move.
The talk shows chimed in with "why is this
Communist on our campus." The English Dept.
grew sick wondering why the poet had come to
town, and without official sanction or invitation.
The Poet-in-Residence at the University shut
his door in our faces and advised us to see him
during office hours. We gave a reading at a coffee
house and Roger, a local poet, was reading about
making it in the back seat of the car. A cop came
to the door and told someone at the door to tell
him to come outside. He told him he couldn't
use that kind of language. All this time Peter was
reading his masturbating poems to the crowd
inside. The cop then took Roger's poems to his
squad car and started reading them to the Chief.
By that time Allen had come out with his Urher
tape recorder over his shoulder, microphone in
hand and told the cop he couldn't take Roger's
poems and to give them back. And the cop was
saying something like he couldn't read them
in a public place. Allen held the mike up and
asked him if he was citing a city ordinance or

what law was he acting under or was he acting on his own judgement, etc. Meanwhile some A.C.L.U. lawyers had arrived along with some of the press. Allen advised the cop to consult his superiors before he got into trouble. The cop radioed his chief who squawked over the radio something like "well they're doing it all over the country not much you can do about it." We went into Oakie's bar and someone sat down next to Julius, who seldom speaks, and thinking he was Allen, he started telling him all about how he had heard of him, etc. Julius got up and silently walked into the women's john and took a piss. It didn't seem to upset the people at Oakie's too much though. Its patrons were kind of an underground in Wichita, in that they didn't belong to the progressive plastic economic trend of the All American City. So Summer or Winter, snowed in, or tornado watch on, there would always be a crowd in Oakie's Bar. Misfits, motorcyclists, lonely aircraft workers from the South, they would all dance jump yell with the band and drink 3.2 beer all night long. It turned out that the patrons of Oakie's were more sophisticated than the University Community, city fathers, art patrons or whatever. The patrons of Oakie's Bar were able to accept someone from a different place. Peter with his hair down to his back. Allen with beard and hair. Julius who never spoke. Oakie's Bar just went right along never overreacting to the new patrons. They were given a big welcome by a barmaid with "Where you all from," and "y'all come back anytime." That was the only honest welcome in Wichita. We drove up to Lincoln, Nebraska and read some poetry on a morning radio show. The engineer's mouth dropped open when Peter said he had been married to Allen for several years. Allen saw the Great Plains and the Vortex and wrote a major poem about it. We went to Menninger's clinic where Allen read, then to a party at one of the staff's houses where Peter took off all his clothes and a doctor's wife flipped out and yelled and screamed that she had seen no one except her husband in the nude. She must have thought Heaven had fallen in.  Allen was the only one around among all those psychiatrists who went over and comforted her and tried to explain things. The party broke up abruptly and I made out with some lady shrink and got on a drunken turnpike to Lawrence with the driver losing the toll ticket and crawling along the nightmare highway under the stars. I fucked her on his living room floor and can't even remember what she looked like. Such was the debauchery of the rainmaker who came to town and fucked all the little girls while riding on the crest of someone else's fame. We went from Lawrence to Kansas City leaving a trail of lust.

After I went back to Wichita, Pam and I got an old truck and went to Lawrence where I wanted to become a junk man but instead worked on Grist Magazine with Fowler and Kimball and got a job at the bean factory to support us. The bean factory was the epitome of what was bad about Kansas labor. After filling out an application with the help of some of the newly acquainted faculty at K.U., who wrote letters of reference for me assuring them I was a good boy and would want to make the bean factory my career, I got a job there. I went to work at 4 p.m. at $1.50 per hour which was very high wages indeed, for Kansas. That included the shift premium of 5 or 10 cents. I went down into the ancient iron catacombs with the boss where creatures from Bosch lugged along, tugging and pushing materials. The bean factory was almost an exception from the bad standards of labor. It was an exception because it was so bad it was almost an art form. It was something like Hieronymus Bosch putting on a happening. Huge vats of pork and bean sauce were on tiers near the roof. Long drains came down into the cans that jumped down the line to get a dash of beans and then a little old lady picked a piece of pork fat out of a tub and plunked it in. Then you had Pork & Beans. A lid was stamped on and these cans would tumble into the hands of two workers who placed them in gigantic iron pots that clanged along on big tongs hooked on to an overhead rail. My job was putting the cans in the pots and pushing them along. Sometimes I would go help stack cases of beans , next to big Joe Palookas. I took the place of a guy who got hit in the head by a case and who had gone to have his eye and forehead stitched up. He returned to work promptly, proudly showing his stitches and going back to work.

–Hey man, why didn't you take the rest of the shift off?

–Na , it wuz nthin. I'se onley gone'bout'n hour.

We ate lunch with a guy who had lost his little finger when putting the beans in the can. He was proud of it. Never tried to collect compensation. The company paid the doc and that was a good deal. I was a good worker and they kept promoting me to better jobs, I guess. It was hard to say for sure. For instance I got promoted to a "Cooker." The young business major foreman told me there was a better job opening. He called me aside and gave me the old pitch saying there's a big turnover of college kids quitting to go to school.

–Do you plan to stay here long? Because if you do, I think I can work you into a better job.

–Well I appreciate that, but as a matter of fact, I was thinking about moving, perhaps next month...

–Oh a month's long enough. C'mon I'll show you what to do.

He took me down to where the big pressure cooker tubs of cans were loaded into by overhead cranes that swung around at the level of your head. I was to close the lid which was a huge plate on an iron screw I turned it around by beating it with a piece of pipe, this fucking lid. Then I would turn on the pressure and time them, then beat that damn screw for all its worth with a iron pipe that was close by. Then I would signal to this dipshit that ran the crane to pick the tubs out. I looked over to this shitface kid who had my job on the other side of the cooling tank.

–This ain't a bad job.

–Naw it ain't too bad.

–I got burned the other night. First degree burns.

He took his shirt off for me to see his back. I started to say, "Gee that's swell," but I couldn't say that. I forgot what I was supposed to say.

–Gee, that's too bad.

–It wasn't too rough though. I was back to

work in three days.

These were hopelessly masochistic slaves who were anti union and wanted to work and work for nothing because work was good. Work meant that you were sober, upright. Work meant that you would not tear your eyes out in a local bar until reality sank back like the dark moon that hung as a reminder of a spirit you may have descended from. Lurking like a spirit of blood, but you sobered up enough to make the job and do your dollar's worth. Hopeless slaves who would like that job no matter if it ate and burned their flesh because at last the Establishment Mother will feel sorry for them. He is a good boy. He carries the burden of the nation in those dragging feet. He has not known  education and has read no books but loves humor in his Daily Grind. He comes to work and clears up the picture of reality from that blackout last night. He carries home his paycheck each week as a badge of merit. There was that pride which carries the nation with his taxes while the Govt. cons him along. Old A.J. Stokely and directors own and control 31 percent common of his life, his sweat, his humor and his ignorance, his fingers and flesh. Sweet masochistic Jesus will sweat his balls off and support the criminal war rather than risk his pitiful world of made over used cars from junk piles. His baloney sandwich. His wiener.

Pretty soon I was asked if I wanted to work overtime. Overtime was time and a half and that amounted to about what a low to normal wage for that part of the country should be. I said I'd stay over and clean the vats. I crawled up on the shakers and cleaned them out with a steam hose and hot water. Some of them had beans sprouting in the dirt that was hard to get to.

–Some of that ole gravy money, now.

–Yeah we're on O.T. now.

Looking in the direction of the clock dragging hoses up to the vats like a tired rat in a cage, I got down inside this vat and washed the sauce out of it. I got to thinking about a joke. It went something like there was this kid whose father owned the company. He was the type of young man who wanted to work up through the ranks. He wanted to start with the lowest job so he would be the best president the company ever had. The foreman agreed and gave him a job cleaning out vats. Years passed and he was still vat cleaning. When the foreman grew older, he told the new workers that this man was the best vat cleaner in the world. That's what I felt like doing the rest of my life, cleaning those vats, hiding from recurring panics. We were all vat cleaners, hiding, hiding from something. What was that vat cleaner over there hiding from? What did or didn't happen in his life that made him content here, tired, whistling until 4 in the morning. The next day I banged hell out of my finger. I went to the foreman and told him I thought my finger was broken.

–Lemme see. OH Naw, that's all right. C'mon... I'll put you over here on an easier job.

He took me to a little room on the side where huge chunks of pork were brought in. I followed the drip thinking what kind of fucking job would he put me in now. He introduced me to a little fellow who made noises down in his throat as he worked. My job was to push big hunks of pork fat into him and he would slice it first one way in several slices and then another, until they were cut up into little chunks. And these were the little delights you come upon in a can of Pork & Beans.

The bell rang for lunch or supper or whatever, and we got our lunches and went back into the room where we worked and moved some pork around and made ourselves comfortable because this is where he seemed to want to eat.

–I like to come in hy'ar to eat.  Some of them go out there. They got some benches in the coffee room.  Some of them go in there to eat. But me, I just come in here.

–Well that way you won't have so far to go when the bell rings.

–Yeah, Huh.

–Yeah, huh.

–How long you been workin' here?

–Goin' on 15 year now.

He unpacked his lunch and brought out a can of pork and beans and opened them and dipped in his spoon.  Oh fuck...  I thought. I had some kind of paranoiac blur of reality. I thought I was paying for Andy Warhol's sins. I knew this little old fucking Fellini creature was going to turn to me and put some far out shit on me.

–Do you like pork & beans?

–Yeah.

–You can get them over at the store they got here for dented up cans. You can gitchyi all kinds of stuff there. Some of the cans fall and they sell 'em to you.  You have to come to work a little early sometime cause it closes at four.

–I'll remember that.

I glanced at the tip of his missing finger and wondered if that old thing about it appearing in the can all started here. Maybe he was the original joke. I felt like I was an eternal joke as I climbed wearily in those bean vats and scrubbed until just before dawn. Each hour I was thinking I might as well keep busy. Keeps me from thinking too much. I looked up at the stars and the tiny lip of dawn, and thought of my sweetheart sleeping over on a borrowed mattress in Fowler's basement with all our belongings arranged on the floor until we got together enough money to get a place. She would model tomorrow and make twice as much in a few hours as I made all night long. And by day Kansas gawked at those who dreamed. Vat cleaners of the world unite! Maybe that is the highest good, just to go around cleaning. Maybe Orlovsky is right. Peter Orlovsky for Janitor of the Universe! But Peter is rewarded by much more than a lowly hourly rate from the millionaire's empire of slaves. Peter cleans because the world is garbage. And the best thing to do is help tidy it up, just this little thing that you can do, which requires a few rags, you can do it. You can give comfort to someone. Perhaps if we all cleaned up for each other as the highest good instead of going to church one Sunday if we all cleaned up the world we could see what each person could contribute. The brothers Orlovsky are the great gurus. One is the guru of cleaning up and the other is the guru of silence, chuckling sometimes to himself about the unknown entities of all possible mobile relationships.

I went to S. Clay Wilson's house. Old red brick with dirt lawns and Harley hogs parked outside.

We took some of his drawings to the old Rock Chalk Cafe and put together a portfolio to print at Fowler's. He was the Aubrey Beardsley of Lawrence drawing hogs, pirates, and tree frog beer. He later became famous for his checkered demon drawings.

The Vortex vibrations were getting too strong so we left for the only place I could call home, SF Golden lights of the Golden Gate through the purple fog of gypsy silk. S. Clay came out there later and homesteaded on 16th. San Francisco is an ethereal city. It's closer to the zoo liquid energy from which all man's essence springs than any other city. Its aura must be grayish purple tonight boiling around the red blue and orange green liquid signs. Like spiritual liquid its energy comes on and off like a neon sign, electrical ecstatic. The ghost of Mammy Pleasant in a voodoo dance off Mission. Old gnarled Eucalyptus hanging their limbs over the Green Eye Hospital. A few blocks in the fog and Glen will be dropping a pill, ready to mount his pony and ride out into that neon grass to hit the stud bars and hard truth movies on a dream, on a dream, on a dream, blasted out of his mind. Up stairs Mag will be zonked out on cheap wine and pot, twisting and shaking with long hair jerking wildly like a hiss in the night. Her hips gathering their own momentum until they move themselves while the Gough St. pad shakes. Behind it clean vinyl fags cruised Jap town with transistors on their wrists, wisping around the corners as easily as the trace of fog. Up the stairs a figure with a cane would slither. An old grey haired man, the great grandson of President Chester Arthur.

He would go upstairs and chart horoscopes. He would keep up with the whereabouts of his astrologically adopted son, Neal. I remember right after the Assassination he was interviewed on the local tube. As he was an Astrologer, he knew that whoever was president was going to die in office. "My friends were appalled," he said, "that I voted for Nixon." Near there, Pat will be painting her monkeys and butterflies amid the collection of old odds and ends piled high in ancient luxury. Out in the streets the fabulous creatures of the night walk in a swish of golden jewelry and bright colored dresses under their trademark, the black leather coat. The skin of black night lit with diamonds. The hickory smoke mixed with the rich flavor of night in the leather seats of the pimp's dented Cadillac. Toward the Haight were the ruins of what was once a nice inexpensive Russian working class neighborhood. Hopeless runaways still arriving searching the street maps in seats of VWs.

There were no more of Dave's soirées. He had been swallowed by a Gurdjieff group and moved out leaving Glen alone in the huge seven room flat. We sat around and talked about the Haight-Ashbury and the changes it had gone through. I thought that hippies were becoming a bore and that hard acid rock at the Fillmore and the Avalon was too loud. I remember walking past a line at the Fillmore several blocks long one New Year's Eve. I had a complimentary pass and didn't bother to go. It wasn't too long ago someone came by Dave's to get him to go down to this little coffee house off Union St. to hear this little group who had a girl singer and called themselves the Jefferson Airplane. Then it kept going and going. Most poets I knew hopped aboard because they had to be into the younger generation. You just about had to say how groovy everything was or be considered old or square. What was there left in SF? It was all the same now. It seemed like I had been on every block, down every St. passed every house. Alan had quit his job at the Oracle as janitor and was about to get in a depression about the whole scene. He had found the eternally young who stayed high and did all the things that excited him a decade ago. Now he felt like he wasn't out of step. Everybody was doing it. Then man's nature began to burn like rubbish until little charred traces remained. The windows in the Haight were boarded up. Fuzzy little dirty girls from Texas and N.Y. walked the pre-dawn streets. What had happened? There were no friends left. Just all new faces and new freaks. The Aquarian Age had blossomed and been sucked up like an egg in a snake's mouth. We found a good place right around the corner from Gough St. One of the last real good rentals left and then the redevelopment bought it. It had been a dance studio. We started having naked parties there. The naked party scene was what I was digging. There were some real big nude parties. And San Gregorio Beach was made into a Free Beach. A public nude beach. That was something to come back to. Hundreds of naked bodies, playing, frolicking in the sun. The office girls from SF playing volleyball with their tits bouncing and pretty snatches gleaming. What a way to spend a day. Only in California! The

Haight burned on. Unbelievably outrageous. The
into outdo and being far out for the fun of it. And
the teenagers moved in. The poets got hooked
on THE YOUNG. And then Pam and I went back
to the Post St. flat. Allen and his family made a
brief visit for the Be-In scheduled to take place
in Golden Gate Park. It was the first of the tribal
gatherings. A man parachuted from the sky and
Allen chanted into the sunset. It was the height
of Haight St. The balloon would burst and there
would be nothing left but Madison Ave. picking
up the rubble. One night the phone rang and I
picked it up and heard this very dignified mellow
opiate voice.

–Hello. This is Herbert Huncke and I'm in
L.A. and supposed to pick up some money from
this gentleman here. As he doesn't know me, I'm
wondering if you'll please identify me. I'll put
him on.

–Sure.

–You see, Allen made arrangements for me to
pick up some bread here so I could come to SF

–Well let me know when you arrive and I'll
meet you. Later we went down to the bus station
in my '48 Plymouth to meet Huncke, Janine, and
Israel.

–Hey man, I dig your car.

He reminded me of a hipster out of the
past. Totally preserved. Here among the whole
panoramic carnival of Hippiedom, the aged
hipster had arrived. There was no way to tell how
old he was. Like an Oriental. Could have been 30
or 60. He wore sport clothes and moved about
in calm efficiency. His hair suggested an ancient
duck tail haircut. He wore a charm or two. The

old captain con man sailed up every river of
life, sold every ticket to the vast side show, the
street corner clairvoyant sniffing out every deal
in town, he wasted no time setting up shop in
SF A sentimental figure out of the past. A real
character was now going to burn the trail of all
the amateurs looking in the windows of head
shops to see what to conform to next. The half-
hip teenyboppers trucking up Van Ness to deaden
their senses with amplifiers at the Avalon while
their grandparents deaden theirs with Geritol
and Lawrence Welk. The half-hip intellectuals
fingering their assortment of phoney drugs as
proud as their suburbanite fathers with their
cars and tractor-mowers. San Francisco was
getting to be a little bit too much. We delivered
Huncke to his destination and went to bed. A few
months later Pam and Janine and I took Huncke
up to the hospital in Mendocino. We got into my
convertible and heard stories until he zonked
out in the front seat.

　–My God! Has he o-deed?

　–No, I don't think so.

　–Let's stop and put the top up.  We might
frighten a motorist and cause an accident.

　–One look at him ...

We stopped and ate some pancakes and
Huncke poured almost all of a jar of syrup on
them. Then he went on the nod with his face
in the pancakes. We got to the hospital and
they weren't going to take him, then I finally
remembered a name of one of their doctors I
knew. We left him there in his new home.

　Bang.  Bang on the door.

–Oh Shit! I didn't go up to see her at the hospital like I promised.

–Chuck! Chuck, open this door. I lost my glasses and purse. I don't know where Frank is. They kicked me out of that goddam fucking Kaiser Hospital. I opened the door and there she stood. A cast on both legs, her slacks torn, her face black and blue, a man's work shirt draped around her. She had been having some of her wino buddies smuggle wine up to her room and they had a party there in the hospital. We gave her a mattress in the extra room and she started recovering enough to start giving orders. Out of the floor full of cigarette butts and a mattress full of wine she began to demand her privileges. Out her window she looked at the back stairs of the Gough St. flat. Neal was going to return there soon very down and very weary. She could have remembered going up the back stairs. Frank coming over that Thanksgiving. A whole big family of cast-offs. Neal running down the halls with his box full of pot rolling joints at phenomenal speed. "Mother Ginsberg" or "Ginzee", Neal would say, would be wiping up the table, making a point, the master of the juicy paranoiac crumb. Sometimes I would think that house was going to lift off the foundation and rise up into the air out of sight.

One night we went to a naked party down in a comfortable little cabin in the redwoods. We were among the first to arrive and the host showed us around. He was a young man in his 20s and worked in some kind of research institute. What else was there around Palo Alto? He was very warm and nice and open and beautiful and wanted everyone to feel the same. He had seen a new world and wanted to show his friends. The cabin was nicely furnished. There was expensive sound equipment with earphones and colored lights plugged into the amplifiers. The lights flashed from the roof and corresponded to the output frequency. The earphones ran into a suspended straw chair shaped like an egg. One guy remarked how sitting in the chair with earphones on was "just like a trip." (What I had to go through just to see some snatch.) I smiled at him and mentioned something about sense deprivation. And he insisted I sit in the damn thing, and try it, exclaiming that it was "too much." He was obviously a crusader for the turned-on generation. I put the phones on and heard some of his bad electronic acid rock. By this time more guests were arriving, a blond chick with long straight hair and white levis, surfer mod, non verbal and smiling always smiling. More were arriving. A big blow up of Tim Leary hung on the wall to greet them. Some of them I recognized from the last party where everyone painted their bodies and danced under the strobe. They danced like a squirming Shiva at a country hoe-down. I was anxious to see all the cunts and cocks beneath all those gorgeous mod outfits, being a pornographer at heart. I asked someone what he was on, just to make conversation, and already anticipated the reply in dope slang, but he answered like a pharmacist going into his whole thing about micrograms and tablets; said most were on acid and I started feeling out of place trying to cover up my boredom, just like at square parties long ago in Wichita.

"Playboy is here," someone whispered. We left right away and drove back to the city. I thought about the drunken Indian who stumbled out on Nude Beach the last time we were there. Every once in a while he would pull his face out of the sand and open his red eyes and try to speak and make motions to the beautiful snatches of the SF secretaries playing volley ball. I wonder if he thought he was in the Garden of Eden. He would try to speak and then his head would fall back in the sand. Was it finally the day the white man promises?We drove back up the coast highway into that serpent jeweled lava city seething in its electric drama visions of lights. What would an old Indian think was going on now, if he had just risen from the ground to look, one who had only known those things of nature that were part of him. Having never touched or seen anything except animals and nature, the stream, the forest, the mountains, only nature, nothing else. How would his eyes interpret the madness of the freeways and city lit up? Would he see it as a vibrating creature from outer space shining and glowing and moving about in the night? Would he think it some electric molten madness that spewed up from the center of the earth? How is civilization seen by an outsider who's never been in contact with it? Is it a mad pit of energy burning itself away? A thing that created and destroyed itself out of a strange flaw in its nature. A thing locked into an endless nightmare of destruction. What does it mean, this thing that chokes itself out of greed and gear? That stockpiles dread diseases? Indian would you build up hordes of anthrax and nerve gases, if you could. Or is no race immune to this flaw of man. Where is the young Indian chemist? The drug that allows memory to see forever. Will there ever be a dream. The kids, they tried, I've got to hand it to them. That Peyote I used to eat in Kansas. I still dream, the green flesh of centuries superimposing itself into the ageless little hunk of acrid flesh. "Man I hear you got some PI-I-OTEE." And when I handed him some he jumped back and looked at this Peyote which was green and wrinkled and grew out of itself: "Man, Hun uh, that stuffs alive," and he took out his handkerchief. But what are drugs but that illegal religion. Legal religion is a stockpile of nerve gas.

Man, the salesman hailing a taxi, a prisoner of a circle of impatience. The hack honking at me to move before the light even changes. I am spurted by his lash of anxiety as a flicker of terror grabs my face dodging autos and the world packed tight from the pages of your life. A manifesto of ashes. S. Clay's checkered demon hitchhiking our of Lawrence, Kansas in Whitman's shorts. Go Find a Johnson.

Betty was in jail down at San Bruno. We went to get her out and took her back to the hotel to get Frank sobered up. He hadn't been out of bed for days. Wine bottles, cigarette butts, and piss all over the floor. Betty went over and cussed him out for not getting her out of jail and then pulled him up, put her arms around him and started singing, "side by side just bummin' around." Frank had just barely enough strength to smile. His lips curled. Soon he would be able to engage in his soft remarkable conversations and read our favorite Fearless Spectator of the Chronicle. His hair was white now and his olive skin wrinkled and scarred. His hands big and gnarled, indicating a lifetime of hard work. He had gone to college up in South Dakota living with a foster family, doing odd jobs to get him through a couple of years. And he got more out of his opportunity at education than anyone I had ever known. He had wisdom. He made use of every little thing that came his way. What a difference, his mind compared to most of the jackass Ph.D.'s. What he could have done with just a little help. There is no justice. But he wasn't bitter toward anyone. He always stood up for the young when guys would get in arguments on the docks. His mother had come to the Dakotas from the South. She was a beautiful black madam who had an affair with the local Irish sheriff. The result was the birth of one of the most beautiful human beings who ever walked the face of the earth. He went to Chicago during the depression and got bum rapped into Joliet. (He was carrying a gat and there had been a robbery somewhere and he was black.) He was in the joint with Leopold and Loeb when one of them was done in. When he got out he went back to South Dakota and got a job as a lineman. He met Betty in a bar in Montana and came back to Oregon with her and stayed at the lumber mill. Then they bummed around together. Picking cherries here, apples there. Back to Denver once or twice. Back to Portland. Finally to San Francisco which was to be home for them too.

I was sick of the pretentious, prudish, hippy cesspool by now. San Francisco had changed. You either had to be mod or hippy or whatever. It was losing its funny character, its feeling. I was sick of SF and of all of California. I didn't fit into what was happening anymore. I didn't care. I didn't try anymore. After Frank sobered up, he got me a job down on the docks and I found a new home. I became a loyal Teamster and worked nights with some of the greatest guys I'd ever met. The Brotherhood convinced me that the poor working stiff can be his own man. These guys didn't take shit from no one. They made you feel like you weren't under the Company's thumb. They were from all walks of life and they were all individuals, loyal to the Brotherhood of Teamsters. I liked it down on the docks unloading freight while the ships sat still with their power plants humming a long voyage drone. Everyone joked all night with each other, trying to get someone keyed up, putting each other on. There was Frank's buddy, a big red-neck from Texas, who Frank called "Big Asshole From Texas," whom everyone would kid about politics. Frank would get him furious, but if Frank got in a jam, the big asshole would be first to help him, and that was how it was. Some longhairs came down to work as extras. The boss picked other guys first and some of the guys said these kids got a right to work too, and forced the Company to put them on. That didn't mean they wouldn't rib hell out of them all night, but that was all part of it. Blacks, Italians, Greeks, Mexicans, Jews, Irishmen, all who had better have a sense of humor because some heavy shit went down, but underneath there was a real sense of brotherhood and if someone challenged that, look out. If the company tried to shit on someone we'd all stop whatever we were doing until it was resolved. That was the job for the "Pineapple", a huge Hawaiian fork lift driver who was one of the Shop Stewards. Most of the talk all night was about politics; some of the younger guys were radical. Frank would always help cool down beefs saying to the boss, "we're always talking about those good old days, and what the hell was so good about them anyway?" There was a Sioux Indian who was from Frank's home town. Once in a while he'd have a little too much like most of us did, and start throwing freight everywhere. One night he was on the bus coming to work with some of us and made us all step out first pointing and saying to each of us, You asshole. You asshole. You asshole. He'd never say much to anyone except me and Frank. I told him I had some Indian blood in me, unless I had a nose bleed. Frank stayed sober and we kept on the job. Betty was getting drunk more often now and was still getting into fights in the Mission St. bars. Things were looking worse for her. When she sobered up she'd go to Sally's and buy a pair of shoes. She'd proudly show us her shoes she had got. The closet was filling up with her second hand shoes. She was getting a little old now to lead such a hard life, but she still left the impression that she could go enough to wear out every pair of those shoes.

So this is where I found a home. On the docks. All that vague past of unknown dream explosions was settling here. Maybe Aquatic Park on a good Sunday where I would remember going there with Alan after those LSD trips from some year past, so vague now, it was either imagined or known, like the great spirit from which all came stuck a vision in my head. This spirit came to earth and attracted the elements to it. Formed a body, like the image in a lamp in water after the water is still from splash. The body complete, the formless fluid energy of thought sought to define itself. o what a task for billions of characters who bounce along in life, not knowing really whether they're in one place or another, or how they got there in the first place. They fill out their lives, incarnate NOW for a certain length of time, their changes as poetic as that ancient game of chance. Their names a muted whisper on the horizon of far away lands: of Peru, or Yucatan, Atlantis or Egypt. Who is this New America? What reincarnated plague, the problems of destruction, like the father before, the civilization before. It speaks of a savior coming. But don't kid yourself. The selfish won't let him. Because the selfish are attached to Material and they have the power of material which destroys the flesh and they are afraid of anything that might interfere with this material into which they've begun to evolve. They will have their God at any cost. And who are the selfish? Anyone who has too much. Anyone who has the power to use other people. America

look to Alcatraz for your freedom! Remember
the Karma of the buffalo and Wounded Knee.

I dug my feet in the sand and looked at
the sailboats on the blue water. They will be
sailing there tomorrow and the next day and
the next. Long after you're gone these little
fortune cookies will float out and out forever.
Something that happened even a month ago is
far back in memory. Everything rushes forward
asserting its own self. Those bongo players, they
will be there again. And the office girls in their
bathing suits. Years become shorter. And right
over there by those benches in the grass that's
where Betty slept one night, she said.

There is Alcatraz, where in 1964 a group of
Indians, citing a 1868 treaty which gave them
the rights to surplus Federal lands, landed on
the island. The papers made fun of it, called
it a "wacky Indian Raid." Remember that San
Franciscans and your Examiner. The Indians
were serious. They had a right to their land.
Could you have a feeling SF like the party in
the canoe felt? No. You have no feeling America,
and you cannot remember feeling until you give
it back. They probably went around the Island
in a triumphal march. Perhaps they made a
circle as the sun set in the western ocean.
Where are your triumphs now? Vietnam? The
broken Indian mends his sorrows and rejoices.
He must have that Island. It is the only karmic
gesture America can make. To give something
back completely. The symbolic token can only
match the Statue of Liberty. The gateway of
the west must be given back in karmic value

the same as the gateway to the east was taken. There was talk of a sculptor making a tribute to the Redman. A million dollar piece of shit. That is what's wrong with America. Always on its terms. Woe to the artist who would dare to put his art there! Or a SF gambling casino. Or tourist traps. If the Island isn't given back, America will have broken its last word. Woe to the contractor who would build on this sacred ground! The cycle is a thousand years coming. There is a permanent jinx for anything that is attempted on Alcatraz, unless it is given back to the Indians. The home of those who murdered, robbed and raped, will be free. The America which murdered, robbed and raped will be doomed, unless this symbolic island is free. It has spoken for all those who have not been treated fair in this country. Take heed America of the Permanent Jinx! Look again at that torch symbolizing hope for the New World! Read the inscription at her feet. The Force of West must give something now. You will again destroy yourself just like those who bum from shore to shore. You will see a stranger walking around Denver, NY, Flagstaff, Barstow or San Bernardino. You will see the Angel Ghost of a broken Indian. You will see Blake's Thirteen Angels. You will see a bum dying. You will see a Sioux woman and her baby shot by a calvary officer, a Vietnamese baby crawling through the jungle of your mind with metal in its flesh, and it will never stop crying. No sirens will drown it out. You are crazy, dazed. You are no longer right. You are the usurper of the world who will

soon devour its own children. You are insane.
You are the Devil acting in the name of Christ.
You do not understand the concept of East and
West. Black and white. Sun and moon. Male
and female. You cannot be loved until you give
back that tiny symbol in the San Francisco Bay.
Only then can you break the mind trap in time
stigmata.

I walked back to Gough St. It was the weekend
and we were still in bed from the long Saturday
night. I had no idea what the loss of one of the
family would be like. The phone rang. It was the
end of the road. She'd gone down so fast. When I
got Frank sober enough to go pick up his check,
he almost cried because the boss said it was the
biggest collection the guys had ever taken up.
I moved on into a stranger world yet, without
someone who had known the past. Neal lay
down by the railroad track. This whole fucking
universe, a stone thrown in the air, people upon
it, pulsating, spinning. Forgotten supernova
shining through the awesome collapse. Those
eyes, as if there is a brighter fluid stirring in
the third brain. The last pair of moccasins and
faded jeans. Invisible partners that may have
disappeared into black holes. Black holes they
say, in the sky. Take a trip into anti-matter. A
copyright on existence. Theoretical residue,
they say, of extremely massive stars whose
thermonuclear fuel has been exhausted. The
fire goes out. If the star is massive enough,
it virtually crushes itself out of existence at the
stellar center. Love, that promising-looking
partner causing celestial donuts on the whole
screen.

Betty had thrown ace/deuce. I was no longer young. Life was falling all around me in a drunken stupor. I laughed and swaggered in ignorance toward the next horizon.

———✳———

# EPILOGUE

## RAPID RONNIE RAP BACK JIVE: 1955

Doc Moonlight bought brand new T-Bird
    from writing scripts
For Bennie-hard bodies dancing.. digging the
    Bebop steps
Long ago Granddaddy bought a paint horse
    in Dodge City
Wyatt Earp' s grandson now sells used cars in
    Wichitity.
Life on the high plains, hot checks & pile of
    loans
Ronnie read hot chicks Pound's Selected
    Poems
Outside Zip's Club smoked boo & pissed
Inside, Pack Rat picked his bass in bliss
His eyes rolled back, into bouncing fret
Scoo bop to do diddy bip bop…next set
From hep to hip cat combo characters sit
Swiiinging go man go! work! bass man star
His nose Inhalers stashed behind the bar
Candy wrappers, cosmos and Benzedrine
Dragnet, luncheonette & make the scene
Play it straight if fate say best stay clean
Really bad,half sad,oh fay,oh say, Ms.O'day
Scuffle on down & slide away from the mass
Wanna smiz -zoke a jiz -ziont of griz -zass?
Rapid Ronnie Rasamutin Runamuck:
Thief, pimp, artists.. hood

Alias Barbital Bob….stood
Under the neon of Zip's Club.
His subterranean boyhood bellhop forays
Found Kansas' big vortex of wild of mores
By the light from the stained glass windows
He drew cartoon characters between shows
He saw all his dreams flyspecked with glory
Filled his pockets with dope & dates of
    whores
And gazed far beyond the gaily painted doors.
Rapid Ronnie rode on the moonlight highs
Pack Rat scoffed pills and played melodic
Drank Oxybiotic that made him neurotic
Jimmy Mammy, just outta the joint, heard
Big Indian was gonna steal Doc's Thunderbird
Ronnie went along reciting Pound's verse
Into the crashing crossroads of the universe.
Big Indian let out a yell of centuries of pain
Drove into the Bulldog's tractor-trailer's lane
Jimmy Mammy broke his jaw & lay in years of
    highs
Ronnie grew old and secret under California
    skies
Big Indian lay dead..his eyes..confused
Staring at the heavens...forever wider
Than the moon's new earth that refused
Him shelter from the great white spider.

# NORTON PRESENTS
# KIM FOWLEY

205

# NECESSARY

## WHILE THEY LAST

Alluring scents for women and men. Generous 1/2 ounce perfume in exquisite glass vial with presentation box.

BILLY THE KID HAD NOTHING ON ME, CUSTER WAS A LOSER TOO

READ BENZEDRINE HIGHWAY BY CHARLES PLYMELL
DISTRIBUTED BY **KICKS BOOKS CO.**
NEW YORK NY USA

**LOSER (BENZEDRINE HIGHWAY)** Hi-octane cocktail for the get-lost generation takes you there and back! With vintage keychain. You supply gas and rod.

**APOCALYPSE ROSE (BENZEDRINE HIGHWAY)** For ladies only- this limited end-times fragrance suggests the nostalgia of undelivered red roses, with bottom notes hinting at a hitchhikers fear of being abandoned in a truckstop lavatory on Route 66. Or possibly, Route 666. You will receive one of four different Roses.

**RAVE (GONE MAN SQUARED)** The world's first beat perfume, a deliciously unsure concoction with hints of coffee and cardamom. Packaged with vintage typewriter key charm.

**SIN TIME (GETTING IN THE WIND)** Venial vixens will find that this exotic elixer evokes excitement at any hour of the day or nite. This big girl scent is equally magnetic for big boys. A pair of tiny dice inside the bottle add a dash to the splash.

**GARBAGE (LORD OF GARBAGE)** The brooding complexity of Kim

## Send All Orders to KICKS BOOKS CO.,

# SPACE IS THE PLACE!
## Sun Ra on Norton

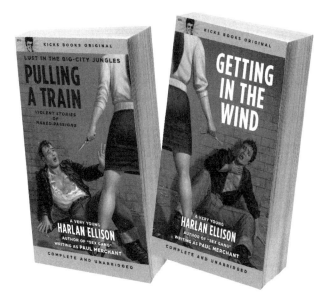

# OTHER KICKS BOOKS
## YOU WILL ENJOY

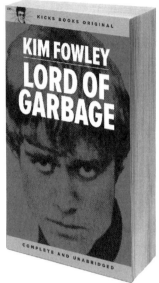

KB1 *Sweets and Other Stories* by Andre Williams
KB2 *This Planet is Doomed* by Sun Ra
KB3 *Save The Last Dance For Satan* by Nick Tosches
KB4 *Pulling A Train* by Harlan Ellison
KB5 *Lord of Garbage* by Kim Fowley
KB6 *Getting in the Wind* by Harlan Ellison
KB7 *Gone Man Squared* by Royston Ellis
KB8 *Benzedrine Highway* by Charles Plymell

### WILLIAMS · SUN RA · TOSCHES
### ELLISON · FOWLEY · ELLIS · PLYMELL

### KICKS BOOKS
PO BOX 646 COOPER STATION,
NEW YORK NY 10276
www.kicksbooks.com